'We are living through times of  –
a global "dark night of the soul"   ds
this terrain. This book guides u   :l,
outlining its background, introd   ı-
aries, from Teresa of Avila to Edɪ... ͻ..ιɪɪ, and inviting us to explore
the Carmelite method of quiet contemplative prayer, just "gazing on
God". A series of very practical contemporary questions encourages
us to apply Carmelite wisdom to our own situations, and allow the
gentle light of Carmel's wisdom to bring insight to our own dark
nights.'
Margaret Silf, author and retreat facilitator

'For any Christians who have asked themselves the question, "How
do I pray?", especially during the sacred season of Lent, this book will
come as a timely help. Father McCaffrey, drawing upon a lifetime's
experience of Carmelite life and his own unsurpassable biblical
scholarship, presents a satisfying synthesis – scholarly and practical,
humble yet brilliant. I warmly commend it.'
Professor Peter Tyler, St Mary's University, Twickenham, London

'Partly because of the intense mystical experiences of individual
Carmelites, and particularly of Teresa of Avila and John of the
Cross, it is too easy to see Carmelite spirituality as "difficult" or even
esoteric; as only suited to very advanced souls. Father McCaffrey
OCD does an extraordinarily lovely job of making this spiritual
tradition somehow "pure" – sensible has become too prosaic a word.
The underlying themes of "openness to the Spirit" through the
Scriptures are made accessible, enriching, worthwhile. It is the sort of
Lent book many of us need – expanding and deepening our practice
as an exploration into the new that, at the same time, has been tested
through the tradition. It is both useful and beautiful.'
Sara Maitland, author of A Book of Silence and many other titles

'In a world marked by division and uncertainty, God calls us to
communion. Too many hearts are beset by lingering weakness and
unhealed wounds. God beckons with silence. Our lives are filled with
the disposable and casual. God entices us with his eternal Presence.
With keen spiritual insight, Father McCaffrey poignantly captures
this spiritual adventure, this journey of accompaniment with the

Holy Spirit, which the Church invites us to set out upon during Lent. With wisdom born of faith, Father McCaffrey delves into the riches of his own Carmelite tradition. His confident assurance is that God is inviting us, yet again this Lent, into a "privileged time for prayer", when the gentle hand of God can transform each of us into the likeness of Jesus Christ.'

Monsignor Joseph Reilly, Rector and Dean of Immaculate Conception Seminary School of Theology, South Orange, New Jersey

James McCaffrey OCD is Director of Teresian Press and Editor of *Mount Carmel: A Review of the Spiritual Life*. He has a doctorate in Scripture from the Biblical Institute, Rome, *The House with Many Rooms: The Temple Theme of Jn. 14.2–3*, and is an experienced speaker on Carmelite spirituality and Scripture. He is the author of numerous publications, including *A Biblical Prayer Journey in the Holy Land*, *The Carmelite Charism: Exploring the Biblical Roots*, *Captive Flames: A Biblical Reading of the Carmelite Saints*, *Prayer – The Heart of the Gospels* and *Infinite Horizons: Scripture through Carmelite Eyes*.

THE WAY OF THE CARMELITES

A prayer journey through Lent

James McCaffrey OCD

First published in Great Britain in 2017

Society for Promoting Christian Knowledge
36 Causton Street
London SW1P 4ST
www.spck.org.uk

For copyright acknowledgements, see p. 87.

British Library Cataloguing-in-Publication Data
A catalogue record for this book is available from the British Library

ISBN 978–0–281–07529–4
eBook ISBN 978–0–281–07530–0

Typeset by Fakenham Prepress Solutions, Fakenham, Norfolk NR21 8NN
First printed in Great Britain by Ashford Colour Press
Subsequently digitally printed in Great Britain

eBook by Fakenham Prepress Solutions, Fakenham, Norfolk NR21 8NN

Produced on paper from sustainable forests

To the memory of my sister Colette

Contents

List of abbreviations and editions used

Works by Teresa of Avila

The Collected Works of St. Teresa of Avila, 3 vols, tr. K. Kavanaugh OCD and O. Rodriguez OCD. ICS Publications, Washington, DC, 1987, 1980 and 1985, including:

F	*The Book of Her Foundations*
IC	*The Interior Castle*
Life	*The Book of Her Life*
Sp Test	*Spiritual Testimonies*
WP	*The Way of Perfection*

Works by John of the Cross

The Collected Works of Saint John of the Cross, tr. K. Kavanaugh OCD and O. Rodriguez OCD. ICS Publications, Washington, DC, 1991, including:

A	*The Ascent of Mount Carmel*
DN	*The Dark Night*
LF	*The Living Flame of Love*
P	*Poetry*
R	*Romances*
SC	*The Spiritual Canticle* (Redaction B)

Works by Thérèse of Lisieux

LC	*St. Thérèse of Lisieux: Her Last Conversations*, tr. J. Clarke OCD. ICS Publications, Washington, DC, 1977
LT	Letters from Thérèse, in *Saint Thérèse of Lisieux: General Correspondence*, 2 vols, tr. J. Clarke OCD. ICS Publications, Washington, DC, 1982 and 1988
PN	*The Poetry of Saint Thérèse of Lisieux*, tr. D. Kinney OCD. ICS Publications, Washington, DC, 1996
SS	*Story of a Soul: The Autobiography of Saint Thérèse of Lisieux*, tr. J. Clarke OCD. ICS Publications, Washington, DC, 1996

Works by Elizabeth of the Trinity

Complete Works of Elizabeth of the Trinity, 2 vols, tr. A. Kane OCD (vol. 1) and A. Englund Nash (vol. 2). ICS Publications, Washington, DC, 1984 and 1995, including:

GV   *The Greatness of Our Vocation*
HF   *Heaven in Faith*
L   *Letters from Carmel [L 84–342]*
LR   *Last Retreat*
PT   *Prayer to the Trinity ['O my God, Trinity whom I adore']*

Works by Edith Stein

HL   *The Hidden Life*, tr. W. Stein. ICS Publications, Washington, DC, 1992
MC   *The Mystery of Christmas: Incarnation and Humanity*, tr. J. Rucker SSJ. Darlington Carmel, 1985 [1985 printing]
Sci Cr *The Science of the Cross*, tr. J. Koeppel OCD. ICS Publications, Washington, DC, 2002
SEL   *Edith Stein: Selected Writings*, tr. S. M. Batzdorff. Templegate, Springfield, Ill., 1990
SP   *Self-Portrait in Letters 1916–1942*, tr. J. Koeppel OCD. ICS Publications, Washington, DC, 1993

Carmelite *Rule*

The Rule of Saint Albert, in J. Malley O Carm, C. Maccise OCD and J. Chalmers O Carm, *In Obsequio Jesu Christi: The Letters of the Superiors General O. Carm. and O.C.D. 1992–2002*. Edizioni OCD, Rome, 2003, pp. 133–9. This edition follows the numbering of points (§) agreed by the O Carm and OCD General Councils and published in 1999: see pp. 127–33 of *In Obsequio Jesu Christi*.

Scripture

Quotations from Scripture are taken and adapted from the Revised Standard Version and the New Jerusalem Bible, with the exception of the Psalms (see below), and passages quoted in the Carmelite *Rule*, for which I follow the translations as in the *Rule* (see above).

Psalms

Numbering and text follow the Grail version, in *The Psalms: A New Translation*. Fontana, London and Glasgow, 1963.

Breviary/Liturgy of the Hours

DO   *Divine Office*, 3 vols. Collins, London and Glasgow, 1974

Vatican documents

References to documents from the Vatican are referred to by section (§) numbers, which are consistent across all published editions and can be found on the Vatican website: www.vatican.va.

A note on ellipses in quotations

Ellipses – seen here as '. . .' – are used both for omissions and also where an author uses them for rhetorical purposes; in the latter case, the abbreviation 'r.e.' (for 'rhetorical ellipsis') will be given in brackets next to the reference for the quotation concerned. Where both types are in the same quotation, the 'r.e.' instance is indicated.

Prologue

My aim, in writing this book, is to explore the spiritual significance of Lent in the company of the Carmelite saints. This is not because they write at length about Lent: in fact they rarely, if ever, speak about Lent – at least not explicitly. And yet, to take up the treasures of Carmelite spirituality, and embark with Jesus on the Lenten experience of forty days in the desert, is a journey that can be enormously enriching and even life-changing. For a Carmelite saint is someone who lives from prayer and the truth of the Scriptures. This book is an attempt, however modest, to help us do the same; it is written not just for Carmelites – members of this religious order which derives its name from Mount Carmel in the Holy Land where it began eight hundred years ago – but for all who wish to be enriched by the spirit of Carmel.[1]

The Gospels tell us that Jesus was led by the Spirit into the wilderness. The scene which then plays out before us is itself rich with references to the word of God. The devil tempts Jesus with a cunning and subtle misuse of the Scriptures. Jesus, in turn, counters with adroit replies in other words of Scripture, in a choice of texts clearly designed to evoke the temptations of God's people on their desert journey: 'Man does not live on bread alone . . . You must honour the Lord your God, him alone must you serve . . . Do not put the Lord your God to the test' (Deut. 8.3; 6.13; 6.16). These replies of Jesus are a reminder to every believer of the power of God's word to overcome temptation.

At the end of the forty days, we are told, Jesus was hungry. Here, especially, his desert experience speaks to us of a God who is eminently human – in touch with his own weakness, and with ours. Jesus reminds us of our weakness (cf. John 15.5) but never promises to remove it. Why? The experience of St Paul helps to shed light on this. Three times, Paul pleaded with God to take away his weakness – Paul's 'thorn in the flesh' (2 Cor. 12.7) – but Jesus answered him: 'My grace is sufficient for you, for my power is made perfect in weakness' (2 Cor. 12.9). Paul accepted this reassurance so much that he would even boast of his weakness: that 'the power of Christ' (2 Cor. 12.9) might be at work in him. 'For the sake of Christ, then,' he declared, 'I am content with weaknesses, insults, hardships, persecutions, and calamities'; and he concluded: 'for when I am weak, then I am strong' (2 Cor. 12.10) – that is, strong with the strength of Christ. This theme, of embracing our weakness so that we may depend totally on God, is one that is typically Carmelite.

The account of the temptations of Jesus concludes with these words: 'when the devil had ended every temptation, he departed from him until an opportune time' (Luke 4.13). Here, the Evangelist is pointing forward to the 'hour' of the passion (cf. Luke 22.53). But even before his passion, Jesus has already won the victory for us. 'The prince of this world is coming,' he says to his disciples, but 'he has no power over me . . . In the world you will have only tribulation, but have confidence because I have overcome the world' (John 14.30; 16.33). The strength of Christ's passion belongs to us already, in union with him. As Paul reminds us: 'Even though it was in weakness that Christ was put to death on the cross, it is by God's power that he lives. In union with him we also are weak; but . . . we shall live with him by God's power' (2 Cor. 13.4).

After the temptations in the desert, we find Jesus returning 'in the power of the Spirit into Galilee' and there proclaiming the word of God by the witness of his life and teaching (Luke 4.14ff.). He shares with others the fruits of his own silence and solitude – from his wilderness experience and his daily times of quiet communion with his Father in prayer. The Carmelite saints can help us to do the same: from their example we learn how we, in our own weakness and vulnerability, may walk this same Lenten journey with Jesus in quiet and prayerful dialogue with God, in the spiritual desert that is so much at the heart of Carmel. We can also learn from them how to listen to the word of God and to shine, by the power of the Holy Spirit, with the borrowed light of Christ – as witnesses in our daily lives to the One who is 'the way, and the truth and the life' (John 14.6).

Therein lies the nucleus of what we will explore in the following pages, in openness to the action of the Spirit: how to *read – and live – the Scriptures* in *the spirit of Carmelite prayer*, with *our eyes fixed on Jesus* who shares with us our weakness, our struggles, our anxieties, our challenges, our temptations. In a word, this concerns everything that is involved in the invitation to take up our cross daily, to follow Jesus through our Lenten experience, and to enter deeply through his passion and death into the joy and glory of the resurrection, guided and strengthened by the Holy Spirit.

With the Carmelite saints, we can strive to bear witness to the truth of Paul's words:

> With Christ I hang upon the cross, and yet I am alive; or rather, not I; it is Christ that lives in me. True, I am living, here and now, this mortal life; but my real life is the faith I have in the Son of God, who loved me, and delivered himself up for me. (Gal. 2.20)

This passage, which speaks of the God who dwells *in* us, and who invites us to *give ourselves as he did*, is profoundly Carmelite.

In the first of the six chapters, we will begin by considering the origins of the Carmelites: not just the location of their first monastery on the remote slopes of Mount Carmel in the Holy Land – an ideal setting for a life of solitary and silent prayer as hermits in community; but, perhaps especially, their *spiritual* origins, as seen in the *Rule*. This text was written, at their request, by Albert, Latin Patriarch of Jerusalem, early in the thirteenth century. But far from being a rigid set of rules and regulations, it is more like a mosaic of scriptural quotations than a legal document. Extremely flexible, and with an inner dynamism in keeping with its words of Scripture, which are abundant, it is capable of growing, expanding and developing under the breath of the Spirit – as it did, so creatively, in response to the changing circumstances of life when the hermits were expelled, soon afterwards, from the Holy Land to Europe. The Carmelite *Rule* is remarkably suited to nourishing us with God's word, so as to foster and deepen a life of silent prayer, whatever our calling may be. It is an invaluable support as we live our Lenten pilgrimage.

In the second chapter, we consider the prophet Elijah, 'Father of all Carmelites', recognizing him to be a great exemplar of contemplation and action. He so often disappears suddenly from the scene to nourish himself in solitude and prayer, and listen to the word God speaks to him – before emerging again, full of fiery zeal, to proclaim that word and call the people of God to conversion. Carmelites look to him as the embodiment of their spirit of *solitary prayer* and their *ministry* that is born from it. The God of Elijah is the 'still, small voice' that *speaks in the silence*. The life of Elijah, like that of Jesus, is a constant reminder to us, during Lent, of the need to withdraw at intervals in the midst of our busy lives for moments of quiet communing with God – moments that will bear fruit in the giving of ourselves in service of others.

While Elijah is considered the 'father' of all Carmelites, Mary is our 'mother' and 'sister'. Indeed, Carmel *belongs to her* – it is the order of 'Our Lady of Mount Carmel'. In our third chapter, we will begin by looking at Mary's integral place in Carmel, before considering her own dispositions in the Gospels as an aid to *lectio divina* – the traditional monastic way of praying the Scriptures – with this incomparable woman of prayer, whom we could rightly call *'the Gospel woman of prayer'.*

We can also turn for guidance, during Lent, to the tradition of prayer embodied in the saints of Carmel. In the fourth chapter, we look first to St Teresa of Avila, the sixteenth-century reformer of the order, and foundress of the 'Discalced' or 'Teresian' branch, which is why Carmelite spirituality is sometimes referred to as 'Teresian spirituality'. Her description of prayer, born of the example of Jesus, is simple and accessible: it is about *friendship with God.* Other outstanding Carmelites, such as Sts John of the Cross and Thérèse of Lisieux, continue the tradition of this 'Doctor of Prayer', complementing her teachings with their own original touch. They, too, will help us to enter deeply into the *desert* of our hearts, to pray and draw life there in the spirit of the Gospels.

In the final two chapters, we focus more specifically on Jesus and the Holy Spirit, in the light of Scripture and the insights of the Carmelite saints. We encounter, here, the means by which our Lenten observance is made possible. In our fifth chapter, we are brought face to face with *the weakness and vulnerability of Jesus*, which is not only scriptural but also one of the most human and appealing aspects of Teresian spirituality. Lent is an invitation and a challenge to journey with the wounded Christ who can show us the truth of our own weakness, insecurity and brokenness, and the truth of a God who is mercy, compassion and tenderness. In the sixth chapter, we have an opportunity to explore some of these most moving Carmelite teachings. We will see, for example, Thérèse of Lisieux speaking to us of the weak, frail and vulnerable Jesus, foretold in Isaiah's prophecy of the Suffering Servant. Akin to this is a particularly moving aspect of Teresian spirituality: the mystery of *God's unrequited love.* The

Carmelite saints point repeatedly to the passion of Jesus as the supreme expression of God's love, rejected and disdained; to a God with arms reaching out to embrace all sinners, 'his heart an open wound with love'.[2] This is a Jesus we can look to with confidence as we carry the burden of our human brokenness, walking with the suffering Jesus by our side – Jesus who is the centre of our lives.

On our Lenten journey, we are always accompanied by the presence of the Holy Spirit who led Jesus into the wilderness and sustained him at all times. In our final chapter, we consider how the Holy Spirit can transform us if we are open to his action. Following the example and teachings of the Carmelite saints, we will learn how to let ourselves be guided by the Holy Spirit in our daily lives and opened up to the work of the Spirit who gives us the light we need in the situations that confront us and the strength we need at times of trial and adversity. Transformed by the Spirit, we will bear witness to Christ in ways more powerful than we could ever have imagined.

Finally, we can never cease to find wisdom in the teaching of the Carmelite saints for our Christian life and for turning the so-called 'ordinary' moments of each day into a life of prayer. To help us to do this – and in line with the practical guidance of the saints – there are questions at the end of each chapter, for discussing, pondering and sharing, which can help us in our daily lives. This is all part of the Lenten experience as we take up our cross daily and follow Jesus – in Lent and every day throughout the year.

1

The Carmelite Rule

A biblical mosaic

All Christians embark on a Lenten journey in preparation for Easter. But before we set out on these forty days of Lent, we should look to Jesus, our model and guide, for direction on the way. After his baptism, we are told, 'the Spirit immediately drove him into the wilderness, and he was in the wilderness forty days, tempted by Satan' (Mark 1.12–13). These words are an invitation to all of us to enter into this desert experience of Jesus and to journey with him on our own Lenten pilgrimage.

This is also a challenge to relive with him the exodus experience of God's people who wandered for forty years in the wilderness on their way to the Promised Land – a time that is consciously echoed in the Gospels by the forty days that Jesus spent in the wilderness. The ideal of the desert, integral to the Carmelite charism, represents a time of total dependence on God and is a source of deep wisdom: 'Remember how the Lord your God led you for forty years in the wilderness,' God said to his people, 'to humble you and to test you and to know your inmost heart' (Deut. 8.2). For help, light and encouragement on this journey, we look to the *Rule* – this invaluable document that has inspired the Carmelite saints and countless others, down through the ages, with its wealth of Scripture and its emphasis on prayer.

A journey into freedom

Those words from Deuteronomy evoke the central experience of Israel's faith: when they were led by God out of Egypt and across the burning sands towards a land flowing with milk and honey (cf. Exod. 3.8). But the exodus is more than a historical event in the distant past. It has always taken on a profound spiritual significance, to designate

1

God's merciful and tender care for his people. It is a reminder to us of how God continues today to guide us all with a loving hand into freedom; our captors are no longer the Pharaohs, of course, but the many sins and attachments that ensnare us. The Psalmist captures the exodus beautifully, as joyful liberation from captivity:

> When the Lord delivered Sion from bondage,
> it seemed like a dream.
> Then was our mouth filled with laughter,
> on our lips there were songs . . .
> What marvels the Lord worked for us!
> Indeed we were glad.
> Deliver us, O Lord, from our bondage
> as streams in dry land.
>
> (Ps. 125.1–4)

If Lent makes us think of an austere, judgemental or frightening God, we need to recall this God of the Psalms who 'delights' in us (cf. Ps. 149.4), the God proclaimed by the prophet Zephaniah: 'he will rejoice over you with happy song, he will renew you by his love, he will dance with shouts of joy for you, as on a day of festival' (Zeph. 3.17). This is encouraging, indeed.

The spirit of Lent

Lent is, of course, a time in which we are called to repentance, self-denial and fasting, but we should preserve at all times a balance and the happy mean. Where the Gospels speak to us of restraint and self-denial, this is not a message of gloom but of joy – the true spirit of Lent: 'When you fast, do not look dismal, like the hypocrites, for they put on a gloomy look, that their fasting may be seen by others' (Matt. 6.16). No, Lent is not a time for gloom and sadness. Most importantly of all, it is a privileged time for prayer – for nurturing our relationship with God – as shown implicitly in this Gospel warning: 'When you pray, you must not be like the hypocrites; for they love to stand and pray in the synagogues and at the street corners, that they may be seen by others' (Matt. 6.5).

The true spirit of Lent is captured in the Carmelite *Rule*, which encourages us to embrace a life of virtue and of intimacy with God. This is a rule that has survived the changes of centuries and still nourishes the spiritual needs of countless women and men, lay and religious, of all ages and nations. The flexibility that this implies requires an adaptable spirit informed by common sense (rather than a rigid attachment to minute details), and in this light its brief conclusion is significant: 'our Lord, at his second coming, will reward anyone who does more than he is obliged to do. See that the bounds of common sense are not exceeded, however, for common sense is the guide of the virtues' (§ 24).

A vineyard of the Lord

The word 'Carmel' denotes the religious and spiritual home of all Carmelites. It is a biblical term derived from a Hebrew word meaning 'vineyard' or 'garden'. When the letter 'l' is added to the word – designating 'El', for the divine Name – it can mean 'the garden [or vineyard] of the Lord'. More accurately, though, it describes a kind of woodland, adorned with a rich variety of shrubs, wild flowers and small trees, much like Mount Carmel today, a prominent landmark in the north of the Holy Land.

The place that is Mount Carmel is referred to in the Bible as a symbol of beauty and fruitfulness, as in the Song of Songs (Song of Solomon), for example, where it is used to praise the beauty of the beloved (cf. Song of Sol. 7.5). It is surely significant that the English word 'Lent' derives from an old English word for the season of 'spring', which is likewise an image that speaks of nature and the beauty of creation. So it is admirably designed to suggest what Lent is really meant to be: a joyful season of rebirth, of new life, of change and transformation after the bleak and lifeless days of winter. This spirit of Lent, too, is evoked beautifully for us in the Song of Songs:

> For see, winter is past,
> the rains are over and gone.
> Flowers are appearing on the earth.
> The season of glad songs has come,
> the cooing of the turtledove is heard in our land.
> The fig tree is forming its first figs
> and the blossoming vines give out their fragrance.
> (Song of Sol. 2.11–13)

Many people today will have heard of the Carmelites, but not all of them may know what it means to be a Carmelite. A Carmelite is essentially *a person of prayer*. We know, of course, that Jesus invites everyone to continual prayer (cf. Luke 18.1). So we may well ask what makes Carmelite prayer so different and unique. To answer this, we must first look back to the origins of the Carmelite way of life, born on the remote and inaccessible heights of Mount Carmel.

The birthplace of Carmel

Towards the end of the twelfth century, a small group of hermits, some of them pilgrims and others crusaders, settled on the slopes of Mount Carmel. This is the mountain range from which the order derives its name: these hermits, then, were the first 'Carmelites'. Traces of their original settlement still survive in the well-preserved ruins of both the monastery and the chapel beside the 'Spring of Elijah' in the wadi 'Ain es Siah. The peaceful valley between quiet, upward-soaring hills kept the minds and hearts of the first Carmelites directed heavenwards and provided them with caves in the rocks, which seemed as if designed by nature to be separate rooms or cells. There, in hushed silence and peaceful solitude, these first hermits could live their lives 'pondering the Lord's law day and night and keeping watch in prayer' (§ 10; cf. Ps. 1.2; Josh. 1.8). These words, to which we will return again and again, are pivotal in the *Rule*: they invite Carmelites to a life of prayer, built on a deep reading and pondering of Scripture. Indeed, as we shall see, *the entire Rule was inspired by the word of God.*[1]

In this same secluded corner of the Holy Land, prayerful eyes could gaze at the vast expanse of the Mediterranean. The hermits would watch the sun set in the glow of twilight and welcome it back at sunrise as it ushered in the dawn of each new day. Everywhere nature spoke to them of God's beauty and power and transcendence, and the boundless ocean opened up for them the fathomless mystery of God's infinite love, with intimations of far horizons reaching into eternity. Here, in this beautiful birthplace of Carmel, 'the heavens proclaim the glory of God' (Ps. 18.2), uniting their silent hymn of praise to the chorus rising up from the praying voices below: 'To him be highest glory and praise for ever' (Dan. 3.57–88; cf. The Jerusalem Bible).[2]

The **Rule** *evolves*

In these idyllic surroundings, the Carmelites lived their daily round of prayer and work as hermits in community, with at that time a limited ministry to others. And so, the Carmelite charism was already a lived experience before ever it became a written document. Early in the thirteenth century, sometime between 1206 and 1214, they asked Albert, Latin Patriarch of Jerusalem, for a rule of life that would be in conformity with the way they were already living. He responded with a fairly brief document, the shortest of all the rules of that time – and one that, perhaps because of this, would prove extremely flexible, adaptable to many life-situations. Despite what the word 'rule' suggests, this text is not a rigid set of rules and regulations. It resembles a mosaic of scriptural quotations and is more like a biblical discourse from Matthew's Gospel than a legal document. Like the Bible itself, it has an inner dynamism capable of growing, expanding and developing under the breath of the Spirit in response to the changing circumstances of the time.

The Carmelites were soon to be uprooted from the Holy Land. Expelled by the Saracens as from 1238, they emigrated to Europe. There, they took on a wider ministry – preaching, teaching and administering the sacraments – and were accepted as one of the new mendicant orders, so-called from the Latin verb *mendicare*, meaning 'to beg'; other such orders, whose members had to beg for their daily needs, were the Franciscans and Dominicans. The way of life of these first Carmelites, during the first forty years of their existence, grew and developed in creative fidelity to the original inspiration of Albert's *Rule*. Now known as the *Primitive Rule of Carmel*, it was given a few modifications, adapting it to the changing conditions of time and place, and this emended document was finally approved by Pope Innocent IV in 1247.

Eyes fixed on Jesus

When discussing a religious rule, it is always good to bear in mind that the Christian faith is *not* primarily about regulations and laws. It is about *the person of Jesus*. We are reminded of this repeatedly in the Scriptures, perhaps nowhere more clearly or simply than when Jesus says: 'I am the way, and the truth, and the life. No one comes to the

Father, but by me' (John 14.6) – for Jesus is the revelation, in person, of the Father. And the author of Hebrews urges us: 'Let us keep our eyes fixed on Jesus' (Heb. 12.2). So we set out on our Lenten journey with our eyes fixed on Jesus, and the Carmelite *Rule* is there to help us do so. For the *Rule*, being steeped in the Scriptures, is centred on Jesus.

The person of Christ embraces the whole of the *Rule*, which can be seen straightaway from its structure and framework. After an initial greeting, 'health in the Lord' (§ 1), we have the phrase 'many and varied are the ways' (§ 2), which echoes the opening of the Letter to the Hebrews (cf. Heb. 1.1), stating God's definitive revelation in his Son. There then follows the main body of the *Rule*, containing several explicit references to Christ and a description of the Carmelite religious life as essentially a following of Christ,[3] which we can legitimately see in its wider sense as the vocation of all the baptized. As the *Rule* gradually unfolds, we encounter the prayer of 'pondering the Lord's law day and night' (§ 10) and note that it is directed implicitly to *the person of Christ who replaces the 'law'* (cf. John 1.17);[4] and the next phrase of this pivotal passage, 'keeping watch in prayer', opens up a further perspective as it suggests the return of Christ at the end of time. This anticipates the end of the *Rule* – 'our Lord, at his second coming' (§ 24) – by which the movement then comes back full circle again, from Christ at the end to Christ at the beginning.

Teeming with Scripture

Albert thought and spoke in biblical terms, and the *Rule* itself, as mentioned, is very much like a mosaic of texts from the Bible – sometimes whole sentences and sometimes isolated phrases which Albert wove together to form his own maxims. The abundance of biblical quotations, both explicit and implicit, at first sight seems disproportionate for a rule so much shorter than its peers. But in its extensive use of biblical references, the Carmelite *Rule* is following in the tradition of St Basil's *Moralia*, a collection of sentences from Scripture which would form the basis of his own rule. Basil did not include one word of his own, believing that any human addition would be superfluous to the word of God.

Still more radically, the desert fathers refused to have a rule altogether: they feared that it could foster servile observance, characteristic of the old law, and thus preclude the freedom of the gospel. Interestingly, this led to their decision to preserve their charism *not by laws but by living examples*.[5] This shows the significance of our charism having begun with the Carmelites themselves – they were a living rule, a living word.

Not surprisingly, the *Rule* encourages Carmelites to steep themselves in Scripture: 'The word of God must abound in your mouths and hearts' (§ 19; cf. Eph. 6.17; Col. 3.16; Rom. 10.8), we read. Or this: 'Let all you do have the Lord's word for accompaniment' (§ 19; cf. Col. 3.17; 1 Cor. 10.31). Teeming with biblical phrases – these last two sentences themselves a mosaic of Scripture – Albert's *Rule* disposes the Carmelite, mind and heart, to be *saturated with Christ's presence through listening to his word*. In addition to the important, focal command to 'ponder the Lord's law day and night' (§ 10), we encounter instances such as: 'listening together . . . to a reading from Holy Scripture', which is prescribed for mealtimes (§ 7); the assurance that 'holy meditation will save you' (§ 19; Prov. 2.11); and a reminder that 'the sword of the Spirit [is] the word of God' (§ 19; Eph. 6.17).

In sum, the Carmelite is referred to 'the Lord's law' (§ 10); to what 'Our Lord says in the gospel' (§ 21); and to the inspired teachings of Paul, 'into whose mouth', we are told, 'Christ put his own words' (§ 20; cf. 2 Cor. 13.3).

A living community

The *Rule* of Carmel prescribes a daily celebration of the Eucharist that binds the religious into a living community gathered around the Lord (§ 14). 'Because there is one bread, we who are many are one body,' Paul tells us, 'for we all partake of the one bread . . . we, though many, are one body in Christ, and individually members one of another' (1 Cor. 10.17; Rom. 12.5). We journey into Lent, not as isolated travellers but as members of a church community, at one with all believers and united with Christ who travels with us.

Albert, we recall, was the Latin Patriarch of Jerusalem, and in his *Rule* he is clearly inspired by the Jerusalem model of the Church in the early chapters of Acts: the sharing and friendship; the joy and freedom; openness and dialogue; the listening to the word; a Church pulsating with the breath of the Spirit, impelling it to growth and expansion. Even a cursory glance at Acts confirms that the community is united 'mind and heart' in the bond of mutual love (cf. Acts 4.32). The primacy of love is everywhere affirmed. The believers are united in this way because 'they devoted themselves to the apostles' teaching and fellowship, to the breaking of bread and the prayers' (Acts 2.42; cf. 2.46–47).

Albert, like Luke, the author of Acts, understands the central importance of the Eucharist. It is a focal point in the community. It involves a prayerful listening to the Scriptures. It is a type of deep prayer, with its still-point in the person of Jesus. It is, most of all, the Presence of Christ.

The strength of a fragile Church

And yet, there is a paradox. We, the members of Christ's Church, strengthened by the Spirit of God, are still broken and vulnerable. When we are beset with temptation, this fragility becomes especially clear. We set out on our Lenten journey, our eyes fixed on Jesus. And this Jesus, who 'can deal gently with the ignorant and wayward, since he himself is beset with weakness' (Heb. 5.2), entered into the depths of human weakness when, in the wilderness, he was 'tempted by the devil' (Mark 1.13).[6]

Temptation is the lot of every Christian. Albert, ever practical and realistic, was only too well aware that the first Carmelite community was a group of weak, struggling and broken members like the universal Church. As mentioned, some of the early hermits had come to the Holy Land as crusaders. This may not seem very 'spiritual', yet a warrior spirit is eminently suited to the Christian journey and is a vital asset, finding its fullest expression in the *spiritual combat*. For these former crusaders, then, the recapture of an earthly Jerusalem was to give way to the conquest of a heavenly one. The way forward was beset with obstacles and called for vigilance and perseverance. Albert quotes Job: 'man's life on earth is a time of trial' (§ 18; Job 7.1). And such a combat requires spiritual weapons – armour of defence, arms of attack – for the devil is always 'on the prowl like a roaring lion,' the *Rule* reminds us, quoting from Scripture (§ 18; 1 Pt 5.8).

For this reason, the Letter to the Ephesians on the spiritual combat is taken up in the *Rule* with striking relevance: 'clothe yourselves in God's armour' (§ 18; Eph. 6.11), Albert writes. The Carmelite community, like that of the early Christians, needed to 'put on' this armour, to use a recurrent expression of St Paul.[7] *Faith* is the 'shield' for all occasions, without which 'there can be no pleasing God,' we are told; and *hope of salvation* is the 'helmet' providing the basis for trust (§ 19). These defences are at the service of communion, directing the Carmelite 'to love the Lord your God with all your heart and soul and strength and your neighbour as yourself' (§ 19; cf. Deut. 6.5; Matt. 19.19; 22.37–39). In this relentless battle, the virtues of faith, hope and love are the strong armour we receive from God and which take pride of place. Our defences are God's gift: he clothes the community with his own strength.

In this light, the spiritual combat is primarily God's work, not ours. However, it is also, of course, closely linked with human endeavour. Even 'work' plays a part in this – it comprises more than a third of the *Rule* – and Albert further links it with silence, for a good reason: 'Sin will not be wanting where there is much talk' (§ 21; Prov. 10.19). The Carmelite is to 'watch and pray' (§ 10), a phrase which immediately evokes the Gethsemane scene: 'Watch and pray that you may not enter into temptation' (Mark 14.38). 'Watch and pray' – alert, vigilant, and always ready to brandish the weapons of God in defence of the Christian life.

Directed in this way by both Scripture and the *Rule*, the Carmelite is called to put on the armour of God like a sentinel on guard, to remain constant in faith, to keep enkindled the flame of love in community – and to rely, in hope, on the promise of a heavenly Jerusalem.

An exodus perspective

There is also a specifically communal dimension in the spiritual defences in Ephesians, from which Albert borrows copiously. The 'cincture' in the armour of God is referred to with these words: 'Your loins are to be girt' (§ 19; cf. Eph. 6.14). At first sight, this suggests the expectant watchfulness of a soldier on guard, and it ties in admirably with the end-time perspective when Albert emphasizes the need to 'keep watch' in prayer (§ 10).

However, the image of the 'girded loins' is also rich in connotations of the exodus meal, which was eaten 'with a girdle around [the] waist' (Exod. 12.11). This evokes the vision of a praying Carmelite community in exile on a collective pilgrimage, faced with obstacles and difficulties but determined to share in the victory of the *new* Passover.

Quite literally, too, this imagery would have had special significance for many of the first hermits who came as pilgrims to the Holy Land, eventually to settle on Mount Carmel. These men were, and would be, often on the move. Their penitential life on Mount Carmel was, in many ways, a continuation of the one on which they had already embarked while in Europe, as part of the movement known as 'The Poor of Christ'.[8] And this imagery would take on additional signifi-cance when the first community was later exiled from the Holy Land and had to continue their pilgrimage and spiritual quest across the sea.

A silent communion of love

An important Carmelite theme that emerges clearly in the *Rule* is *solitude* – hence, the recurrent aspects of prayer, keeping watch, silence, separate cells. The ultimate purpose of all these things is inner transformation. We asked earlier what it is that makes Carmelite prayer unique. And this is what gives it its distinctive stamp: *an intimate sharing alone with God*, in a *silent communion of love, open to the transforming action of the Spirit.*

To enable this to happen within us, the Carmelite is called to be a *hermit at heart*. This is significant: it means that anyone and everyone, whatever their state in life, can live in the spirit of Carmel – by becoming a Carmelite *in their heart*. At the outset of the *Rule*, Albert directs the Carmelite to Jesus and to serving Christ faithfully, 'pure in heart' (§ 2; cf. 1 Tim. 1.5). The word 'heart'[9] speaks of an inner space, a place of the utmost silence and receptivity to God's presence, whether in the Eucharist, in prayerful communing with God, or in absorbing the Scriptures with the word of God 'abounding in our mouths and hearts' (cf. § 19; Col. 3.16; Rom. 10.8).

Allied to solitude is *silence*. Here, Albert was highly original. For within the tradition of religious life, there is no other rule that reserves, comparatively speaking, so much space for silence. This is all the more significant as Albert, who is so succinct on other themes, is expansive on this one.

If we look again at the central section – on staying in one's cell and pondering the Lord's law day and night (§ 10) – we find one single sentence, describing four basic exercises: remaining, pondering, watching and praying. Silence, of course, is an aid to these things and does not outweigh them in importance. But it is still quite remarkable that the theme of silence (§ 21) has two hundred and ninety-nine words devoted to it! (Faith, hope and love have only seventy-two.) Moreover, Albert is especially astute and discerning in his choice of Scripture texts in support of silence. He takes, for example, a cluster of passages, such as Isaiah 32.17, Ecclesiasticus 28.26 or Matthew 12.36, all of which combine to stress the spiritual combat, with a view to intimacy and quiet communion alone with God.

The heart of the eremitical life, however, is more than silence itself: rather, *silence is the atmosphere that must envelop it.* It is, likewise, more than the solitary cell. We are not dealing here with just a physical place: the cell is equally meant to be seen as the visible symbol of *the inner shrine of our heart,* in which dwells the risen Christ. And in this inner cell, we need to make ever-increasing space for God as we 'keep watch in prayer' (§ 10) and await his 'second coming' (§ 24).

The 'work' of holiness

The instruction to Carmelites to remain in their cell, 'pondering the Lord's law', contains a significant exception: 'unless attending to some other duty' (§ 10). This 'duty' or work is not specified: the main thing is that Albert urges Carmelites not to be idle 'so that the devil may always find you busy' (§ 20). And Pope Innocent IV added this comment summing up the whole section on work: 'That is the way of holiness and goodness: see that you follow it' (§ 20; cf. Isa. 30.21).

This additional phrase, expressed in a way that is both general and inspiring, mirrors the flexibility of the *Rule.* It reminds us, yet again, that we do not have to be in a monastery to live the Carmelite life: we simply need to have diligence (or 'lack of idleness') and to place our work at the service of 'holiness' and 'goodness'. Albert is drawing on St Paul when he says: 'Let all you do have the Lord's word for accompaniment' (§ 19; cf. Col. 3.17; 1 Cor. 10.31).

For the early Carmelites themselves, their active work had begun with a limited amount of preaching to pilgrims and other people, but it became a full ministry after they were exiled to Europe. The point of gravity now shifted from the countryside to the cities. And it was most likely as an adaptation to the pressing demands of the Carmelites' new lifestyle that Pope Innocent IV modified the *Rule* to reduce the time of nocturnal silence.

What can we learn from the *Rule* for our own life and work? We learn, first of all – as in this reduction of nocturnal silence – not to compromise on prayer, while at the same time avoiding any rigidity in observance that would be incompatible with the work we are called to do and our service of others. We also need to bear in mind that the *Rule* encapsulates the three main elements of the religious way of life – the eremitical, community life, and the apostolic dimension – and that we need to hold them in a fruitful balance. The *Rule*'s flexibility allows these to take on greater or lesser priority, according to the changing circumstances of life, but if one of the three disappears altogether, the essence of the Carmelite charism is lost.

For the early Carmelites, exiled to Europe, the *Rule* showed them that it did not matter whether a monastery was located on Mount Carmel or across the seas, in a solitary place or in a city, provided it was essentially *a true Carmel* – where solitary prayer, fraternal love, and ministry to others were inseparably linked.

Moving with the Spirit

The greeting of Albert at the beginning of the *Rule*, 'blessing of the Holy Spirit' (§ 1), is not a mere greeting but would also seem to be designed precisely for that very purpose: to dispose the recipients of the *Rule* for *openness to the Spirit*. By the last line of the *Rule*, Albert can withdraw from the scene, his work of capturing the charism complete. For the rest, a vast silence, like the silence of the Gospels, descends and opens up a space for the work of the Holy Spirit. Quickened by the Spirit, the *Rule* becomes a many-faceted text, always open to deeper understanding like the Gospels, and admitting new forms of Carmelite life in response to the 'signs of the times'.

Jesus says to us, in John: '[The Spirit] will remind you of all I have said to you' (John 14.26). If we read these words in reference to the *Rule*, this would not be just a reminder of the letter of the law or even, if we may say this, of the spirit of the law as such. Rather, the Holy Spirit will point out the *relevance of the text here and now* as time unfolds.

The silence of the blank page, once the *Rule* has ended, carries the same message as Jesus in the Gospels: 'I have yet many things to say to you, but you cannot bear them now' (John 16.12). The *Rule*, too, awaits the further light of the Spirit. 'He will declare to you the things that are to come' (John 16.13), we are also told in the Gospels, as Jesus announces the coming of the Spirit. This perspective widens into an unknown future of growth, expansion and development. It is the same Spirit who will lead us into all truth (cf. John 16.13) – into the full richness of a charism that not even the most definitive rule can adequately express in words. It is a charism that continues to unfold.

The universal family of Carmel – to which we might also add the many non-Carmelites who draw inspiration from its spirit and teaching – is spread throughout the world with many varied expressions of its charism, for men and women, friars, nuns and lay people.[10] Each branch of Carmel, even each community, has its own differences of emphasis. But each lifestyle is the fruit of a profound and prayerful listening to the word of God and to the *Rule*, in the light of the Spirit. All Carmelites look to the future to discern where the Spirit is sending them, in the hope of doing ever more for the Church. *This* is the 'more', the 'over and above', of which the *Rule* speaks in its closing lines. The Church is filled with the wonders of the Spirit, who 'breathes where it wills' (John 3.8). We must be ready at all times to expect the unexpected from God.

Questions for reflection or discussion

1 If you had to write a rule of life for yourself, based on your favourite passages from the Scriptures, what would it be?

2 What does it mean for you 'to meditate on the law of the Lord day and night'?

3 How can the Carmelite *Rule* help you in your life of prayer?

2

The heritage of Elijah
Father of all Carmelites

Unlike other religious families, the Carmelites have no founder or foundress as such. The Teresian branch of the order was founded in the sixteenth century by Teresa of Avila, along with her companion John of the Cross. It is, though, perhaps more accurate to see them first and foremost as *reformers*.[1] If asked about their roots – their identity and spirituality, what we refer to as their 'charism' – the early Carmelites would not have been able to name a saint such as Benedict or Francis of Assisi. They would simply have turned to Elijah – known as the 'Father of all Carmelites' – whose story is explored in this chapter.

The exploits of this great prophet still clung like sacred memories to the mountain that, we have seen, is Carmel's origin: Mount Carmel in the Holy Land. The 'spring of Elijah', referred to in the *Rule* (§ 1), evokes a long oral tradition centred on this great prophet who is now, in a real sense, father and founder of Carmel as we strive to live in his spirit. It is to this fiery prophet that the first Carmelites looked for inspiration and the embodiment of their vision and ideals.[2]

We read, in Ecclesiasticus, these inspiring words: 'Elijah arose like a fire, his word burning like a torch' (Ecclus. 48.1). They are emblazoned beneath a statue of Elijah at Muhraqa, 'The Place of Sacrifice', on the eastern slopes of Mount Carmel. This powerful figure stands with flaming sword raised aloft, a vanquished false prophet beneath his feet, and his eyes reaching out across an endless plain as if to proclaim a message relevant for all people and all time.

Man of prayer, man of action

Elijah might well serve as a model and guide for all believers as we embark on our Lenten pilgrimage of faith. Lent is a time of repentance, conversion and renewal. And Elijah calls us to repentance, conversion and renewal – just as he once called the people of God, with a clarion cry, to return to their faith in the one true God of the covenant.

Lent is also a special time for renewed commitment to prayer. Here, too, Elijah is an outstanding model. He is a great contemplative who provides a witness to perseverance in prayer and, indeed, to the deepest form of prayer: *contemplation*, which is so embedded in the Carmelite tradition. Contemplation, as we might describe it, is a silent, loving glance towards God in faith and simplicity, with our heart open to receive God's gift of himself. John of the Cross expresses it beautifully when he writes: 'pure contemplation lies in receiving' (LF 3:36) and when he gives us this now classic definition: 'contemplation is nothing else than a secret and peaceful and loving inflow of God, which, if not hampered, fires the soul in the spirit of love' (1DN 10:6).[3] Elijah, as a man of prayer, felt himself constantly called into silence and solitude, yet was repeatedly summoned out of his solitude to proclaim the word of God. This paradox is ample proof, if it were needed, that God gives true contemplatives a great love for silence and solitude but does not always grant it.

We should note, too, that Elijah was no stranger to failure, loneliness, despair, powerlessness and even apparent abandonment in his relationship with God. He can teach all of us on our Lenten journey that God's grace is sufficient for us, that his power is made perfect in our weakness, and that when we are weak then we are strong (cf. 2 Cor. 12.9–10).

When Elijah first appears on the stage of history, like a thunderbolt, to announce a drought, he gives these stark credentials: 'As the Lord the God of Israel lives, in whose presence I stand . . .' (1 Kings 17.1). He will later describe his sense of mission by saying: 'With zeal have I been zealous for the Lord, the God of hosts' (1 Kings 19.10, 14) – words that adorn the Carmelite crest. This prophet, a challenging role model for all Carmelites, comes across as a vigorous personality, yet he is always one of depth and contrasts – appearing suddenly, only to disappear again just as suddenly as he retreats into solitude: a man of action and a man of prayer. It is not surprising that Carmelites find in him an exemplar of their spirit and mission for today's world, as well as the roots and offshoots of Carmelite spirituality.[4]

A journey of the heart

The Carmelite way is a journey of the heart, moving ever closer towards encounter with the living God. This implies moving away from our selfishness and from all that keeps us from God. It is in this sense that the Carmelite journey is like the exodus experience of God's people and their meeting with God in the wilderness. On their desert march, the Israelites encounter a transcendent God who challenges them with the radical demands of his covenant: 'I am the Lord your God, who brought you out of the land of Egypt . . . You shall have no other gods before me' (Exod. 20.2–3).

Salvation history repeats itself in the story of Elijah. The prophet confronts the wayward people of his day with these same radical demands. He sees them wavering, dithering, 'hobbling now on one foot, now on another' (1 Kings 18.21) as they vacillate and yield to the lure of false gods. So he challenges them to conversion with these clear and uncompromising words: 'If the Lord is God, follow him; but if Baal, then follow him' (1 Kings 18.21). Elijah then calls on God to rain down fire and set the sacrifice alight. On seeing the miraculous work of God, the people make a choice as clear and uncompromising as Elijah's challenge had been: 'The Lord, he is God; the Lord, he is God' (1 Kings 18.39).

Carmel, too, demands that God be at the centre of our heart. But while these demands are radical, they are never rigid or insensitive. Carmel's call to us is like falling in love: meeting someone special who captivates us and enkindles a passion deeper than other, lesser, loves. Once God is at the centre of our heart, all those other affections fall gradually into place. It is like discovering the 'pearl of great price', the 'treasure hidden in a field' (Matt. 13.44–45). All this is simply a question of priorities: 'You shall love the Lord your God with all your heart, with all your soul, and with all your might' (Deut. 6.5). And St Paul expresses the fullness of the challenge when he writes: 'what we have to do is to give up everything that does not lead to God' (Titus 2.12).

Carmelites, and all who live in the spirit of Carmel, are called to search in every dark and hidden crevice of their heart for those lurking demons of Israel's desert experience: the 'venomous serpents and scorpions' (Deut. 8.15) inhabiting the wilderness.[5] They represent our false gods, like the 'baals' or idols worshipped

16

by the false prophets in Elijah's day. For us, these idols may take the form of the snares of worldly attachments, our disordered or inordinate desires, and all the things unrelated to God that have become non-negotiables in our lives. We must *never* replace God with our idols, or act as if they were more important to us than God. The Carmelite way is a journey *into* God with the freedom of an undivided heart. 'God alone suffices,' as Teresa tells us.[6] God alone can satisfy our deepest hunger.

Standing before the face of God

As Carmelite spirituality is essentially about prayer, Elijah holds a very special place for us as the great contemplative. In a passage already seen – and all the more significant for being Elijah's first appearance – the prophet describes his own personal relationship with God: 'As the Lord the God of Israel lives, in whose presence I stand . . .' (1 Kings 17.1; cf. 18.15). This is, quite literally, contemplative: always he *stands before the face of the living God* – his prayer is a gazing on the face of God.[7] This will reach its most profound expression when God passes before Elijah on Mount Horeb.

Before Elijah's intense encounter with God on Mount Horeb, however, the spirit of the prophet had first to be refined and tempered in solitude at the brook Cherith.[8] It is also at this time that the wayward people become disposed for God's intervention by three years of parched waiting during the drought. When they finally face Elijah at the place of the sacrifice, a dramatic contest ensues. Elijah addresses the God of the covenant – the One who is always pursuing his people *in search of their love*: 'let this people know that you, O Lord, are God and are winning back their hearts' (1 Kings 18.37). Carmelites, too, emphasize prayer as *a response to love*.

Elijah's prayer stands out in striking contrast to that of the false prophets of Baal. Their antics are, indeed, a parody of true prayer. Howling and shrieking, they limp around the altar they have constructed, hurling empty phrases at the silent heavens, gashing themselves with swords and lances – while Elijah taunts them, mocking their so-called god: 'Perhaps he is asleep?' (1 Kings 18.27), he enquires! Jesus warns against the kind of prayer that uses an abundance of unthinking words: 'Do not babble, as the pagans do, for they think that they will be heard for their many words' (Matt. 6.7). Prayer is not bombarding God with our requests – using an avalanche of words or pious formulas to try and bend his will to ours. Prayer is just the opposite: it is surrendering our will to *God's* will. Or, as expressed so well by the character of C. S. Lewis in the play *Shadowlands*: '[Prayer] doesn't change God. It changes me.'[9]

Transforming prayer

To be changed, to become transformed, is one of the greatest emphases of Carmelite prayer. This is, as said before, an affair of the heart. It is the *new* heart – that is, the *transformed* heart – promised to us by God in the books of the prophets: 'I will put my law within them, and I will write it upon their hearts . . . A new heart I will give you, and a new spirit I will put within you' (Jer. 31.33; Ezek. 36.26). Prayer is the life of this new heart.

For Carmelites, the heart is the 'inner room' where Jesus invites his disciples to pray: 'When you pray, go into your room and shut the door and pray to your Father who is in secret' (Matt. 6.6). Prayer – and the transformation it brings – requires extended periods of time, as it did for Jesus. It also demands special conditions: silence, solitude, withdrawal into the secret oratory of a quiet heart. In the words of Dietrich Bonhoeffer, the great Lutheran theologian who, incidentally, felt an affinity with John of the Cross: 'Teaching about Christ begins in silence.'[10] This is just as true of Carmelite teachings: before we can share with others a teaching about God or about prayer, we need a prolonged and silent communing of love with God in the depths of our heart, so that we become the person we need to be, if our teaching is to bear fruit. The Australian poet James McAuley captures the transforming effect of this quiet prayer of faith:

> Incarnate Word, in whom all nature lives,
> Cast flame upon the earth: raise up contemplatives
> Among us, men who walk within the fire
> Of ceaseless prayer, impetuous desire.
> Set pools of silence in this thirsty land . . .
> Prayer has an influence we cannot mark,
> It works unseen like radium in the dark.[11]

Into the dark night

We recall once more the dramatic conflict on Mount Carmel between Elijah and the followers of Baal. As we have seen, his challenge to them is radical: there can be no compromise with false gods. Elijah can call the wavering people to conversion because he is confident that God himself is 'turning back their hearts' (1 Kings 18.37). And so the drama unfolds. Yet the same prophet, who successfully urges others to conversion, must in turn experience conversion himself. This brings us to a phenomenon that is most closely associated with the teachings of John of the Cross: the 'dark night'.

Immediately after the people turn back to God, we might imagine that Elijah rejoices at this victory. Far from it. He now withdraws into solitude, fleeing the infamous Jezebel who had championed the false prophets. Elijah journeys back into the desert – and into himself – as if tracing in reverse the exodus experience of the people of God. Here, we are about to see that this great prophet was 'as frail as ourselves' (Jas. 5.17), in the words of the apostle James.

In the wilderness, Elijah sounds the depths of human weakness. He enters a spiritual dark night and sits despondent amid the debris that is, he feels, his life's achievement.[12] This crushing experience wrenches from him an agonizing prayer: 'It is enough; now, O Lord, take away my life; for I am no better than my fathers' (1 Kings 19.4). This experience of desolation has its own important place in the Carmelite prayer journey. Here, Elijah experiences the depths to which God will go to seek out the human spirit, in order to sear it and enkindle in it the fire of his love. This is the God of the burning bush at work in the darkness of faith – our God who is 'a consuming fire' (Deut. 4.24; cf. Heb. 12.29). Layer upon layer of selfishness is peeled away under God's purifying touch, and this cleanses the spirit like fire that chars and blackens before the wood can finally glow like the living flame that consumes it. With this suffering, the temptation to return to the 'flesh pots of Egypt' (cf. Exod. 16.3) and to abandon prayer altogether becomes more pressing than ever.

Here, in his dark hole of despair, Elijah is fed by an angel. There, he tastes the heavenly 'manna'. This great prophet, who has always been alert to the word of God, is now called to a listening deeper than ever before. Humbled, softened, purified and refined through apparent failure and seeming abandonment by the Lord, he is about to discover a new face of the living God. He journeys, with hope, 'in the strength of that food forty days and forty nights to Horeb' (1 Kings 19.8) – 'the mountain of God'.[13]

When God speaks in the silence

'What are you doing here, Elijah?' (1 Kings 19.9). After this question, which comes from the Lord himself, the prophet is then told: 'Go out and stand upon the mountain before the Lord' (1 Kings 19.11). There, it will not be in the elements – the wind, the earthquake, the fire – that the Lord is to be found, as he was in the thunder and lightning and dark cloud on the heights of Sinai (cf. Exod. 19.16; Heb. 12.18). But then, after all the noise and commotion on Horeb, suddenly all becomes quiet – and Elijah encounters the God of the gentle breeze, a 'still, small voice' that speaks in 'the rustling of a light silence' (1 Kings 19.12), whispering softly with the breath of God.[14] For Elijah, and for all who truly pray, *God speaks in the silence*.[15]

No 'graven image or likeness' can ever represent the transcendent God of Israel's story. He remains for ever the Unknown Stranger who constantly withdraws into the hidden quiet of his own mystery (cf. Gen. 32.22ff.). This is why the prayer of *faith* is so important – for faith *believes* even though it cannot *see* (cf. John 20.29). Carmelites are summoned to listen constantly to the word of God in faith, 'pondering the Lord's law day and night', as the heart of the *Rule* enjoins, and 'keeping watch in prayer' (§ 10). No wonder Elijah is a model for every Carmelite – called to be alert to the word God speaks in the silence of prayer; called to be vigilant, like a watch in the night.

To 'watch and pray' – this takes us to the agony of Jesus, who warns his disciples in Gethsemane: 'Watch and pray, that you may not enter into temptation' (Matt. 26.41). But this battle does not apply only to critical moments in our lives. As the *Rule* reminds us, in the words of Job, 'life on earth is a time of trial' (§ 18; Job 7.1). A Carmelite is called to battle for and with the Lord, as Elijah did.

The prophetic element of Carmel

And Elijah will battle, one more time, against the powers of darkness: for this great prophet is thought to appear for the last time in the

Scriptures as a martyr and witness in the final onslaught of Satan (cf. Rev. 11.4–13). Edith Stein refers to this tradition when she writes: 'According to the testimony of the Book of Revelation, [Elijah] will return near the end of the world to suffer a martyr's death for his Lord in the battle against the Antichrist' (HL, p. 3).[16]

To witness is itself to be a prophet, in that our words and our lives *speak to others of God*. The wiles of the evil one are insidious. So, the *Rule* of Carmel calls us to *vigilance*, to *prayer*, and to *witness to others* and even disturb them, if need be, by witness to our values; to be ready to be rejected, as Elijah was, in challenging the conscience of our times: 'Is it you,' King Ahab greeted Elijah, 'you troubler of Israel?' (1 Kings 18.17).[17]

This is the prophetic element in Carmelite spirituality, embedded in its charism. So here, too, we are called to take Elijah as a model, in order to hear the word of God deep within ourselves and to share it with others. For a Carmelite, to 'keep watch in prayer' is to be always on guard, like the prophet Habakkuk 'standing on the watchtower' (Hab. 2.1); to be always, like Elijah, standing faithfully in prayer before the face of the living God, asking in the prophet's words 'that this people may know that you, O Lord, are God' (1 Kings 18.37); and witnessing to others, in the conflict between good and evil, prompting them to respond like the people of Elijah's day: 'The Lord, he is God; the Lord, he is God' (1 Kings 18.39).

Contemplation and action

Undoubtedly, Elijah is a man of stunning exploits. He raises a widow's son to life (1 Kings 17.17–24). He defeats the prophets of Baal, after the mighty contest on Mount Carmel (1 Kings 18.20–40).[18] And he counters corruption, in the episode of Naboth's vineyard, which shows Elijah's concern for social justice (1 Kings 21). Yet this outstanding man of action is primarily a *listener*: alert, persevering, attentive in his listening to the word of God.

We find a recurring pattern in the prophet's life: withdrawal into solitude followed by intense activity. This is a telling proof of the quiet space which Elijah *needed*, for *listening to the word before he proclaimed it* with his powerful words and mighty deeds in the Lord's name. It was just the same for Jesus, too. As Carmel teaches, contemplation is not the opposite of action: it is its *source* – the perennial spring of all fruitful action and ministry.

The story of Elijah ends with God's command: 'Go, return on your way' (1 Kings 19.15). His solitude was not an escape, like a permanent retirement. Instead, he was drawn into God *only to go out of himself* and so embrace the service of others again, in a whole new way. Neither does a Carmelite choose solitude to escape the challenges of life. Prayer is never a selfish flight from the call of duty or from the grind of daily living. In silence, Carmelites listen more intently, and with compassion, to the pain of the world; even for those who have entered a monastery, the neediness of the world they have left behind is where the compassionate core of their heart continues to live.

To return from the 'Tabor' of deep silence and prayer is to return to the world with a heightened awareness of one's mission. In this way, we are called to relive the Gospel account of the Transfiguration, so conducive to silence and deep contemplation: for from the heights of Mount Tabor, the disciples are enjoined by Jesus not to ignore the vast plains lying beneath – mission fields 'already white for the harvest' (John 4.35), as we read in John's Gospel. So, too, Elijah's encounter with God on Horeb is, literally and spiritually, a peak experience, not a journey's end. And so, when the Lord commands him, 'Go, and return on your way', he immediately informs Elijah of his future mission (1 Kings 19.15–18). The prophet, transformed by his encounter with God on Mount Horeb, now returns to the previous theatre of his activity, able to share with the people the fruits of this deep encounter with God.

A new face of God

Elijah first appeared unexpectedly; and at the end he disappears unexpectedly, mysteriously carried up into heaven by 'a chariot of fire and horses of fire' (2 Kings 2.11). But his spirit remains in the lives and ministries of countless Carmelites throughout the world who wish to follow in his footsteps and proclaim his message to a needy world – to people who are still hungry, however unconsciously, for purpose and meaning in their lives. Carmelite spirituality, inspired by Elijah, answers to the deepest longing for love in every human heart: the yearning to be loved, to be *set ablaze* with love. John of the Cross speaks of the person being transformed by the flame of the Holy Spirit like wood transformed by fire (cf. 2DN 10:1; LF 1:3–4); and Thérèse prays that the Spirit will transform her into fire (cf. SS, p. 195). This is an echo of the Song of Songs:

> Love is strong as Death,
> passion as relentless as Sheol.
> The flash of it is a flash of fire,
> a flame of Yahweh himself.
>   (Song of Sol. 8.6)

Carmel is all about that flame, the ever-living and unquenchable flame of God's eternal love for us, the fire that blazed in the heart of Elijah – the fire of the Holy Spirit that sets our own spirit on fire.

Questions for reflection or discussion

1 What idols do you have in your life, of which perhaps you have not been aware?

2 Take one difficult experience from which, like Elijah, you have emerged not broken but renewed. In what way did adversity become a means of growth?

3 How can the experience of Elijah help you in your prayer?

3

Reading the Scriptures with Mary
An invitation to lectio divina

Linked inseparably with Elijah in the Carmelite tradition is Mary, mother of Jesus, who may be called 'the Gospel woman of prayer'. Already in the late twelfth century, a chapel was dedicated to her as part of the first Carmelite community on Mount Carmel itself; the ruins remain to this day. Early Carmelites simply called Mary 'Carmelite' – in other words, 'one of us!' Today, too, Carmelites see themselves as Mary's sisters and brothers, an invitation open to all. And for the presence of Mary in the founding of Carmel, we need to consider another aspect of the story of Elijah.

After the conflict with the false prophets of Baal had ended, we find Elijah, true father of all Carmelites, at prayer: he 'climbed to the top of Carmel and bowed down to the earth, putting his face between his knees' (1 Kings 18.42). Then his servant, keeping watch, called out to him: 'Behold, a little cloud like a man's hand is rising out of the sea' (1 Kings 18.44) – a harbinger of the rain about to fall in torrents, an answer to prayer after three years of drought. In the mystical memory of Carmel, this 'cloud' is seen as a symbol of the mother of Jesus. But why?

The answer does not, in fact, point to some kind of insubstantial myth. Titus Brandsma, a heroic Carmelite priest killed at Dachau, draws attention to the symbolic import of this cloud for Carmelites. He refers to passages in the Old Testament, such as that of the cloud that overshadowed the Ark of the Covenant in the wilderness, and shows that a cloud was often *the sign of God's presence among his people*.[1] Carmelites see the cloud rising from the sea as a symbol of Mary's place in the mystery of the Incarnation – bearing Christ and bringing him to us – which is fully in harmony with the Old Testament as a foreshadowing of the New. To borrow the words of St Paul: 'the reality is Christ' (Col. 2.17).

24

From the beginnings of Carmel, then, Mary has been an essential presence. Carmel belongs to her – it is the Order of 'Our Lady of Mount Carmel'. Her presence, as our mother and sister, is also that of a *woman of silent prayer*. In this way, she has always been a vital inspiration to Carmel, integral to its charism; and it is as a witness to prayer that we will consider Mary in this chapter.

With the heart of Mary

Everyone wishing to embark on the Lenten pilgrimage in the spirit of Carmel would be well advised to do so with Mary as friend and companion, and with a Bible in hand – and heart. To read the word of God in the spirit of Carmel is to pray it with the heart of Mary: it is to put on the dispositions of her inner life, knowing that she, more than anyone, listened to and welcomed the word of God.

Mary is a living witness to the quiet workings of God's grace within her as she responds, in the concrete circumstances of her life, to the challenge of his word. A glance at her life provides us with some aids that we all need, for a simple and renewed approach to reading the Scriptures in a way easily accessible to all. At the same time, we will draw on the wisdom of the age-old practice of *lectio divina*, with its four traditional stages.[2] We will look, in this chapter, at the prayer of Mary as a model for our own *lectio divina* – a way of listening prayerfully to the word, and responding with our lives.

Essential dispositions

There are no barriers when Mary listens to the word. There must be none for us, either. She is *at ease*, reassured when the angel tells her not to be afraid – aware that she is the object of God's special love. This *awareness of his love for us* must also be our own entry point into prayer – for we, too, 'have found favour with God' (cf. Luke 1.30). We must *stand before God just as we are* – like Mary who said to the angel, 'Behold, I am the handmaid of the Lord' (Luke 1.38).

God looks on his servant 'in her lowliness' (Luke 1.48); and with this in mind *we come as weak, frail, vulnerable and contrite sinners*, unmasked before a God whose 'mercy is from age to age' (Luke 1.50). Mary comes before him, knowing that he who is almighty has done – and can still do – great things for her. We, too, must start with that same *attitude of trust* and be *ready to risk everything on the truth of his word.*

Let us listen to the word, be challenged and surrender ourselves to it. If we wish, we can do all this with an eloquently simple gesture of empty and upturned hands – waiting to receive whatever God wishes to say to us and ask of us.

Open to the Spirit in faith

We begin by invoking the Holy Spirit. For this, we may choose a prayer of our own liking. Perhaps it will be a traditional, simple invocation, such as, 'Come, Holy Spirit.' Or if we prefer, we can of course formulate a prayer in our own words. Reading the Gospels, open with Mary to the action of the Spirit, will centre us directly on her Son. We must always bear in mind that the inspired texts, those of both the Old Testament and the New, *speak of Jesus*. So, we focus on Jesus, together with Mary who was the first to fix her eyes on the Word made flesh. As John of the Cross wrote so beautifully: 'The Mother gazed in sheer wonder' (R 9). He was contemplating with the eyes of Mary, and to see through her eyes is to see Jesus.

Mary sees through *faith*, and it is her faith that unlocks the real secret of her approach to the word of God. Her cousin Elizabeth recognizes this, saying: 'Blessed is she who believed that the word spoken to her by the Lord would be fulfilled' (Luke 1.45). We, too, must come to each text of Scripture in a spirit of faith – a faith like Mary's, ever searching for a deeper meaning and understanding of what God is doing, here and now, in our lives. So we come to Scripture, making an act of faith, opening our inner eye to the action of the Spirit who will 'come upon' us as he did for Mary (cf. Luke 1.35).

Pondering in our hearts

We now *read* the word. We select a short passage and repeat it slowly, more than once, reflecting on it and listening to it deep within our hearts. We wait for a word or phrase to stand out for us from the page.

We then *meditate* on these words, like Mary 'pondering them in our heart' (cf. Luke 2.19, 51). Perhaps the most mysterious and challenging of all the messages she received from God is this: 'You will conceive in your womb and bear a son . . .' (Luke 1.31). Her heart would immediately have begun to ponder their meaning, trying to fathom their unfathomable depths.

When we, too, are seeking to understand the meaning of the word of God, light begins to dawn when we call to mind *other words of Scripture*. So, when the angel says to Mary, 'the Lord God will give to him the throne of his ancestor David' (Luke 1.32), this refers back to the Old Testament prophecy that will now be fulfilled: Mary's Son will be the promised King-Messiah and Son of God, sprung from the house of David (cf. 2 Sam. 7.12–14). We can be enriched and enlightened very deeply by pondering on the word of God in this way: for, how often a word of Scripture is sparked off for us and clarified by associations with other words of the Bible. We do not need to go in search of them; a listening heart will simply receive them. We let them come spontaneously, unbidden.

When we ponder the word, we also read it with our *life's experience* and let our life's experience be read by it in turn. This often painful journey takes us into the very core of our being. But gradually, this *will* bear fruit, and enable us to become, ourselves, a living word. This has nothing to do with sublime heights beyond our reach. Rather, it is the effect of direct contact with the power of God's saving love, released through the word by the Holy Spirit. It is love, and love alone, that can change and transform us. The word touches our heart, and we let our hearts go out in love. The word of God is descending from our head to our heart.

Out of the depths of the heart

In response to this movement of the heart, we now begin to *pray* the word. We lay bare before the Lord whatever surfaces for us from it: our aspirations and longings, our disappointments and hopes, our concerns and gratitude, our joys and sorrows – all rising up from the wellsprings of our heart. We speak to God and tell him our inmost thoughts and desires. Sharing with him our needs, and the needs of others, is to follow the example of the Virgin at Cana who merely stated the problem to Jesus, then trusted him to provide the solution. 'They have no wine' (John 2.3), she said simply.

We must not be shy about exposing to God our worries, our questions, even our doubts. For even though he knows them already, he wants us to tell him about them – to treat him as a 'friend', as Teresa would say, in line with Jesus himself (cf. *Life* 8:5; John 15.15). Like Mary, we will surely feel bewildered and confused at times. 'How can this be?' (Luke 1.34), she asked the angel. And on another occasion we are told that she 'did not understand the saying' (Luke 2.50). Perhaps we may be wrestling with an urgent problem, seeking an answer that never seems to come. Then we can recall Mary's question to Jesus: 'Why have you done this to us? Your father and I have been searching for you anxiously' (Luke 2.48).

As we walk in the light of the word, we will find a new self-knowledge; we will be content, like Mary, in our 'lowliness' (Luke 1.48) as we discover a God of mercy who exalts the humble. When this happens, we will find ourselves brimming with thanksgiving and praise, and we will resonate with these words of Mary who exclaimed: 'The Almighty has done great things for me, and holy is his name' (Luke 1.49). Again like Mary, we can give ourselves over to an inner current of joy, remembering her cry of delight: 'My spirit rejoices in God, my Saviour' (Luke 1.47).

A simple gaze of love

As our prayer continues, we may notice that it gives way to a deep stillness. Exultation becomes calm and focused. Now is not the time to be *doing* things in prayer. In peace and confidence, we must let ourselves be drawn into this stillness – into what is nothing less than the eloquent silence of *contemplation*. While this term has traditionally been thought by many to be lofty and outside our reach, it is in fact nothing more, and nothing less, than a *simple gaze of love towards Jesus*, with an *openness to the gift of God himself.*[3]

In spirit we will stand with Mary, gazing on her Son, just as she herself stood at the foot of the cross, communing with him in love. And in this gaze we will receive into our open hearts the gift of Jesus himself. This is what is meant when John of the Cross, penetrating the heart of the mystery, writes, as we have seen: 'pure contemplation lies in receiving' (LF 3:36) and is 'a secret and peaceful and loving inflow of God, which, if not hampered, fires the soul in the spirit of love' (1DN 10:6).

Responding with our 'yes'

In the heart of the stillness, and in a very subtle way, God will inspire us with what he wants us to do. Our first response is one of disposition. This takes us again to Mary gazing on her Son at the foot of the cross, for there she received her mission to be mother of the Church: 'Behold your son' (John 19.26), Jesus said to her, looking on the Beloved Disciple who represents all of us, all the members of Christ's Church. To *accept the word* spoken to us in Scripture or in the silence of contemplation is to respond to God's invitation to us with Mary's *fiat* – her 'yes'. This is her *surrender to God's will*; and we, like her, must say: 'Let it be done unto me according to your word' (Luke 1.38).

It is vital that we make Mary's 'yes' to the word of God our own, even when the page before us does not immediately 'speak' to us. It may be that the seed of the word is still sinking into the soil of our hearts. We have only to be patient: it will thrust up its shoots at the proper time. This can be a slow, gradual, almost imperceptible process. The spiritual life is, in any case, a marathon, not a sprint: we must walk at God's pace, as Mary did when puzzling over the angel's enigmatic message and awaiting its unfolding in God's own time.

Even when God seems to be silent, we must not anticipate his action but must remain always open to its fulfilment. We need constancy, determination and resolve in this desert experience – and the 'desert', too, as said before, is at the heart of the Carmelite charism. We need to hold firm, as Mary did, when her initial *fiat* received its ultimate testing on Calvary. All we have to do is trust in the goodness and wisdom of God, knowing by faith that his word will bear fruit at the appointed time. To recall this prophecy of the Lord, given to us in Isaiah: 'the word that goes forth from my mouth does not return to me empty, without carrying out my will and succeeding in what it was sent to do' (Isa. 55.11).

Doers of the word

We have responded to God's word with an inner and committed 'yes'. The fruit of this prayerful surrender to God's action through our immersion in Scripture is *our action*, in response to his word. Action can take many forms, as many as the needs to which we are called to respond. But Mary's experience shows that they will be essentially the same for us as for her:

- *Compassion*: hurrying to our neighbour in need, just as Mary 'arose and went with haste into the hill country, to a city of Judah' (Luke 1.39), so as to tend to her cousin Elizabeth.
- *Witness*: inviting others to come and listen to Jesus, saying to them in the words of Mary at Cana, 'Do whatever he tells you' (John 2.5), and announcing to the world the wonders of God's goodness, as in this marvellous line of the Magnificat, 'My soul proclaims the greatness of the Lord' (Luke 1.46).
- *Solidarity with the community of believers*: as we pray, for them and with them, together with the mother of God and mother of the Church – Mary, who was 'joined in continuous prayer' (Acts 1.14) with the first disciples. We wait, like them, for the outpouring of the Holy Spirit who will bring back to our memory the word we have read – the word spoken by Mary's Son, for the building up of the Church and for the service of our neighbour.

Ultimately, to listen to the word of God is to be conformed to Jesus who 'went down with [his parents] to Nazareth and was obedient' (Luke 2.51) – 'obedient', in the radical sense of the term which is nothing other than 'listening'.[4] Mary listened to Jesus, and he listened to her. That is what reading the Scriptures in the spirit of Carmel should mean for all of us, during Lent and at all times: a perfect dialogue of love.

Questions for reflection or discussion

1 What aspects of the life of Mary can help you in the concrete circumstances of your daily life?

2 The early Carmelites described Mary as their sister. Think how you might 'take her into your home', as did the Beloved Disciple, and how you might live in companionship with her.

3 In what ways can the example of Mary show you how to embrace contemplative prayer?

4

Teresian spirituality
A life of prayer

———◦◦◦———

Lent is a special time of prayer. It challenges us to enter, with our eyes fixed on Jesus, deep into the desert of our own heart, to pray there in the spirit of the Gospels. On our Lenten journey, we cannot do better than turn for help and light to the saints of Carmel. For the Carmelite tradition itself might be called a tradition of prayer.

It is good to begin by looking to St Teresa of Avila (1515–82), known as the 'Doctor of Prayer'. It is to her that every Carmelite turns for light and inspiration, so as to learn how to commune with God in the true spirit of Carmel. Her description of prayer is clear and simple: it is about *friendship with God.* Indeed, her genius for friendship conditioned her whole teaching on prayer. What is perhaps most remarkable, however – given the limited access to the Bible in her day – is the scriptural depth contained in her works. The teaching of Teresa is firmly rooted in the word of God; indeed, it is like an epitome of the Gospel teaching on prayer. Like Jesus, Teresa bears witness to prayer by both word and example.

Jesus – our Friend

For Teresa, Jesus is always the focus of prayer, and her eyes are always fixed on him. She writes:

> I see clearly . . . that God desires that if we are going to please Him and receive His great favours, we must do so through the most sacred humanity of Christ . . . Many, many times have I perceived this truth through experience. The Lord has told it to me. I have definitely seen that we must enter by this gate . . . desire no other path even if you are at the summit of contemplation; on this road you walk safely. This Lord of ours is the one through whom all

31

> blessings come to us . . . In beholding His life we find that He is the
> best example. *(Life* 22:6–7)

In earlier times, Teresa had made the mistake of following certain authors who advised praying to God in what might be called a purely spiritual way, without reference to the God-made-man – 'the sacred humanity', as she often expresses it. But this mistake, which later she deeply regretted, was to prove a happy fault. It would have unique significance for her later teaching. Afterwards, she never ceased to warn others against the dangers of withdrawing from the incarnate Word at any stage on the spiritual path. For beginners: 'The soul can place itself in the presence of Christ . . . This is an excellent way of making progress, and in a very short time' *(Life* 12:2). And for the more advanced: the failure to keep Christ present as a model, she says, 'is why many souls . . . do not advance further or attain a very great freedom of spirit' *(Life* 22:5). Moreover, there is an essential link between the mystery of Christ and the greatest grace of all, in prayer: the spiritual marriage, which importantly was given to Teresa through the sacred humanity of Jesus (cf. IC VI:7:6). It is no surprise that one of her favourite Gospel texts was: 'I am the way, and the truth, and the life' (John 14.6).

'An intimate sharing between friends'

In the eighth chapter of *The Book of Her Life*, Teresa gives us a now famous description of prayer, which strongly emphasizes prayer as friendship with God. She introduces the passage with these words: 'I trust then in the mercy of God, who never fails to repay anyone who has taken Him for a friend' *(Life* 8:5). She concludes it with this exclamation of praise: 'Oh, what a good friend You make, my Lord!' *(Life* 8:6). And this is the kernel of her description, which contains all the essential ingredients of Teresian prayer:

> mental prayer in my opinion is nothing else than an intimate sharing
> between friends; it means taking time frequently to be alone with Him
> who we know loves us. *(Life* 8:5)[1]

This celebrated description of prayer speaks of what is central to Teresian prayer – *the intimate sharing between friends* – and highlights the conditions of *time*, *space* and *solitude* for this friendship to persevere and grow.

Turned 'towards' the Father

The intimate sharing between Jesus and his Father – who he knows loves him (cf. *Life* 8:5) – is the perfect model of the friendship and companionship to which Teresa invites everyone in prayer. In the story of her life, she recounts a vision she had, showing her 'that the humanity [of Jesus] was taken into the bosom of the Father' (*Life* 38:17). This was a privileged insight into the truth of John's words: 'The only Son, who is in the bosom of the Father, he has made him known' (John 1.18). This image is used in Scripture for the closest and most tender of human relationships: that of mother and child (Ps. 130.2; cf. Num. 11.12), of husband and wife (Deut. 13.6), and also of friends, like the beloved disciple reclining on the 'breast' of Jesus at the Last Supper (John 13.23).[2] It describes an intimate friendship of love.

The exact form of John's original words (cf. John 1.18) is quite stunning. The phrase is not strictly '*in* the bosom' but '*into* the bosom' (*eis*, in the Greek original) – a word that conveys, as it were, both rest and motion: a timeless relationship between Father and Son, already accomplished; and at the same time a ceaseless and dynamic thrust between the two.[3]

'He first loved us'

At the Last Supper, Jesus speaks to his disciples as 'friends': 'I have called you friends . . . You did not choose me, but I chose you' (John 15.15–16). For love and friendship go hand in hand: 'No one has greater love than this, to lay down one's life for one's friends' (John 15.13). The important thing to note is that Jesus was about to lay down his life for his disciples, *not because* they were *already* his friends, but *in order that* all might *become* his friends. Paul expresses the idea perfectly: 'God shows his love for us in that while we were yet sinners Christ died for us' (Rom. 5.8).

Jesus is offering us a closeness and intimacy with himself, and this automatically invites a response: 'God is love . . . We love, because he first loved us' (1 John 4.16, 19). For Teresa, *prayer* is this response. It is not a technique, not a means of self-fulfilment: as Teresa shows us again and again, prayer is an active engagement in friendship with God.

'This little heaven of our soul'

When Teresa describes prayer as 'an intimate sharing', she is repeating in her own way the lesson of Jesus in the Sermon on the Mount: 'When you pray, go into your room and shut the door and pray to your Father who is in secret; and your Father who sees in secret will reward you' (Matt. 6.6). In the Carmelite tradition, this 'room' is also – and especially – understood as the *inner room*: what Teresa calls 'this little heaven of our soul'. It is there, in the depths of our heart, that she, like Jesus, invites us to share with God in prayer:

> Those who . . . can enclose themselves within this little heaven of our soul, where the Maker of heaven and earth is present, and grow accustomed to refusing to be where the exterior senses in their distraction have gone or look in that direction should believe they are following an excellent path and that they will not fail to drink water from the fount; for they will journey far in a short time. Their situation is like that of a person who travels by ship; with a little wind he reaches the end of his journey in a few days. But those who go by land take longer.
>
> (WP 28:5)

This secret communion with God 'does not lie in thinking much', Teresa tells us, 'but in loving much' (cf. F 5:2; IC IV:1:7). It releases God's love, given to us at baptism when it was 'poured out in our hearts by the Holy Spirit who has been given to us' (Rom. 5.5) – active in us as the power of God's love reaching out to others in the new commandment for us to 'love one another as Christ has loved us' (cf. John 15.12). This love, already promised in the prophets as a 'law within' (Jer. 31.33), 'a new heart' and 'a new spirit' (Ezek. 36.26), is a 'law', St Paul tells us, 'written . . . with the Spirit of the living God . . . on tablets of human hearts' (2 Cor. 3.3). It is a love given by God in response to the prayer of Jesus: 'that the love with which you [Father] have loved me may be in [my disciples]' (John 17.26).

Jesus invites his disciples at the Last Supper to 'abide' in this love (cf. John 15.9–10) – permanently, intimately united to himself. It is a covenant of friendship that is deeper, even, than the love of Jonathan for David: 'The soul of Jonathan was knit to the soul of David . . . Then Jonathan made a covenant with David, because he loved him as his own soul' (1 Sam. 18.1, 3).

Alone with 'the Alone'

Special conditions are required for authentic prayer, as we note from these words in Teresa's description of prayer: 'taking time frequently to be alone' (*Life* 8:5). Each element of this phrase is important for friendship with God to grow and deepen: we need *time* to pray, perseverance so as to pray *frequently*, and a space for solitude where we can be *alone* with God.

The example and teaching of Jesus are a perfect example of these conditions. Luke, especially, refers to the prolonged *time* that Jesus spends in prayer, when he tells us that on one occasion Jesus 'spent all night in prayer to God' (Luke 6.12); and in Gethsemane, in his agony, he prayed 'more earnestly' or 'at greater length' (Luke 22.44). We also see Jesus spending time alone at prayer just before he teaches his disciples the Our Father (Luke 11.1), as well as at some of the great turning points in the unfolding of God's plan of salvation – at the choice of the Twelve (Luke 6.12), on his manifestation as Messiah (Luke 9.18), and at the Transfiguration which prepares the disciples for his passion (Luke 9.28–29).

So, too, we often see Jesus *alone* with his Father and sharing with his disciples his *preference for withdrawal from the crowd*, as in this passage in Mark where Jesus invites them to 'come away by [themselves] to a lonely place and rest awhile' (Mark 6.31). In an earlier episode, Mark's first description of Jesus' silent prayer does not, significantly, refer to just an isolated incident but designates what happens at the beginning of *a typical day* in the ministry of Jesus: 'in the morning, a great while before day, [Jesus] rose and went out to a lonely place, and there he prayed' (Mark 1.35).[4] Luke, too, reminds us that this quiet prayer of Jesus occurred constantly during his life: 'he withdrew to the wilderness and prayed' (Luke 5.16) – literally, 'he used to withdraw', repeatedly, into a remote place for quiet prayer. Likewise, when Luke records the solitary prayer of Jesus on the Mount of Olives, he states explicitly that Jesus went there with his disciples 'as was his custom' (Luke 22.39); Jesus had, then, already prayed in that place very frequently with his followers.

To pray *frequently*, we must persevere, even when we may not feel like it. And if we feel that our prayer is achieving nothing – whether spiritual growth or what we call 'an answer to prayer' – we should act like the importunate friend who comes at midnight and knocks incessantly until his request is granted (cf. Luke 11.5–8). Jesus reinforces this lesson with another parable, that of the widow who pleads incessantly with a judge for redress (cf. Luke 18.1–8), a story introduced with these challenging and encouraging words: '[We] ought always to pray and not lose heart' (Luke 18.1).

The preference of Jesus for the isolation of mountain and hillside, the lonely desert places and the stillness of the night, and for long periods of time, day after day – all this lends support to Teresa's explanation of prayer as 'taking time frequently to be alone' with God. It shows her teaching to be deeply embedded in the Gospels and confirmed by the example of Jesus himself. It is hardly surprising that she had a particular love for those Gospel scenes where Jesus is alone at prayer. More exactly, she wished to be *alone* just to be *with* Jesus – 'alone with the Alone', as it is often expressed. So Teresa represented Christ within her 'in those scenes where I saw Him more alone. It seemed to me that being alone and afflicted, as a person in need, He had to accept me. I had many simple thoughts like these' (*Life* 9:4).

A long and painful struggle

Teresa's life was an adventure in prayer. She does not speculate about prayer; she communicates her own experience of it and freely invites us to share in this ourselves. But her prayer journey was not a smooth passage from first fervour to mystical heights. Her growth in prayer would prove to be a long and painful struggle.

To speak with God as with a friend did not come easily to Teresa at first. A long 'at first': in fact, it was the fruit of nearly two decades of intense 'aridity' in prayer – a state in which consolations in prayer are lacking – although these years were relieved at intervals by some consolations and even brief periods of deep mystical prayer. Teresa's thoughts wandered uncontrollably 'like little moths at night, bothersome and annoying' (*Life* 17:6) and she was unable to reason, think or meditate, or picture any scenes to herself in God's presence. She felt powerless for no less than 'eighteen years', of which she writes:

> In all those years, except for the time after Communion, I never dared
> to begin prayer without a book . . . For the dryness . . . was always felt
> when I was without a book. Then my soul was thrown into confusion
> and my thoughts ran wild. (*Life* 4:9)

She confessed how, during these years of crisis, she used to wait
anxiously 'for the striking of the clock' to end the hour of prayer, and
how she had to 'force' herself to persevere (*Life* 8:7).

Her 'temptation of Judas'

During this troublesome period, Teresa experienced an additional
crisis. She was becoming ill at ease with some of her friendships and
infidelities in her life. She realized that her prayer and lifestyle were
not in harmony. This discrepancy began to disturb her greatly and
discouraged her from praying. In fact, at one stage she even gave up
prayer altogether (cf. *Life* 7:11; 19:4).

Teresa did, however, return to prayer after abandoning it 'for a year
and a half' or, at any rate, 'at least for a year' (*Life* 19:4). She described
the infidelity of giving up prayer as the beginning of the temptation
of Judas (cf. *Life* 19:11). When this trial was over, she would continue
in her earlier resolve. But her unhappy experience was to prove
a blessing in disguise and to leave a lasting impression. Later, she
would repeatedly caution others against the dangers of abandoning
prayer. Moreover, her method for perseverance during her trials was
simple but effective. It is also highly beneficial for those who are
eager to understand the Teresian way of communing with God and
to advance in it, as we shall now see.

Representing Christ within

During her long years of wrestling with wandering thoughts, Teresa
followed a helpful device: what she calls *representing* Christ as near,
or within her, where she could speak to him. It grew out of frustrating
beginnings, the inability to represent Christ in the Gospels with
either her intellect or her imagination:

> I had such little ability to represent things with my intellect that if I
> hadn't seen the things my imagination was not of use to me, as it is to
> other persons who can imagine things and thus recollect themselves.

> I could only think about Christ as He was as man, but never in such a way that I could picture Him within myself . . .   (*Life* 9:6)

This was a painful experience for Teresa, as she longed to establish a real personal relationship with Jesus and to commune with him, near to her or present within her. So she pressed into service every ruse she could conceive of, such as reading a book or identifying with her favourite characters in Gospel scenes. Eventually, she discovered the key – she *represented* Christ *within*:

> I tried as hard as I could to keep Jesus Christ, our God and our Lord, present within me, and that was my way of prayer. If I reflected upon some phrase of His Passion, I represented Him to myself interiorly . . . God didn't give me talent for discursive thought or for a profitable use of the imagination. In fact, my imagination is so dull that I never succeeded even to think about and represent in my mind – as hard as I tried – the humanity of the Lord . . . This is the method of prayer I then used: since I could not reflect discursively with the intellect, I strove to represent Christ within me . . .   (*Life* 4:7; 9:4)

A presence in faith

At a first reading, Teresa seems to contradict herself: she cannot picture Christ within herself, so she *represents* him within herself instead. However, the phrase, 'to represent Christ within', can have a twofold meaning. It can, of course, denote picturing him with the imagination, but it can also signify *re*-presenting him: in the sense of *making him present again*. This is Teresa's use of the word. At prayer, she did not 'imagine' Christ, nor could she ever do so. She strove to 're-present' him to herself: to make him present to herself *in faith* – that is, to *become aware, through faith, of his presence* – as Someone who *really was present* within her, not just as an image:

> I was like those who are blind or in darkness; they speak with a person and see that that person is with them because they know with certainty that the other is there (I mean they understand and *believe* this, but they do not see the other) . . .   (*Life* 9:6; italics mine)

There is nothing here resembling the Ignatian method, however valuable in itself, of setting a scene and imagining, for example, what the incarnate Word looked like. Teresa just makes space within herself for Jesus in his sacred humanity, and enters her 'inner room' where she can be 'with him' and 'in him', and he in turn be 'with her' and 'in her'. Here, they can talk and commune together in that 'intimate sharing between friends' which is Teresian prayer.

Teresa's attempt to make Jesus, in this way, *present again through faith* is in line with what Jesus describes as the 'recalling' action of the Spirit (cf. John 14.26). The Spirit makes Jesus present again, alive and active here and now in the heart of the believer, and relevant to the challenge of living the gospel values in the concrete circumstances of every Christian life.

The prayer of recollection

Silent communion with God who is within us is often referred to as the *prayer of indwelling* – so called because our soul is a dwelling place for the Lord (cf. John 14.23; 15.4; 1 Cor. 6.19; 2 Cor. 6.16). It is a hallmark of Carmelite prayer. Closely allied to this focus is a method of prayer particularly associated with Teresa: the *prayer of recollection*. Here, the faculties are gathered together, focusing on that indwelling presence of God in the soul. We will now look at Teresa's own description of recollection.[5]

'I confess', Teresa writes, 'that I never knew what it was to pray with satisfaction until the Lord taught me this method' (WP 29:7). This 'method' is recollection, and Teresa is speaking here about silent prayer in the presence of God. Some people consider this to be independent of vocal prayer, and even superior to it. Yet, as Teresa shows, vocal prayer is intimately linked with recollection: 'With this method', she assures us, 'we shall pray vocally with much calm, and any difficulty will be removed . . . get used to praying the Our Father with this recollection, and you will see the benefit before long' (WP 29:6).

Recollection, then, can and should inform all prayer, whether silent or vocal. It involves a double movement on our part: focusing on Christ in our prayer, and entering into ourselves to be with him when we pray. We might call this a perfect response to the Gospel text, 'Where your treasure is, there will your heart be also' (Matt. 6.21).

Remain there in his presence

All Teresa's advice is designed to simplify the tangle of what is known as 'discursive meditation' – reflecting with the mind or intellect – and so calm the distractions of too much thinking. Christ is really present, which is why recollection is sometimes called 'the prayer of presence'; it has also been called 'the prayer of companionship' and is closely allied to 'centring prayer'. We have only to look at Jesus, or see him looking at us – and listen to what he has to teach us. To *look at him* with a simple and intuitive gaze of faith and love – this is the kernel of Teresa's advice, as in these two passages:

> one should . . . just remain there in His presence with the intellect quiet . . . occupy ourselves in looking at Christ who is looking at us, and . . . speak, and petition, and humble ourselves, and delight in the Lord's presence . . .   (*Life* 13:22)

> behold Him on the way to the garden . . . Or behold Him bound to the column . . . Or behold Him burdened with the cross . . . He will look at you with those eyes so beautiful and compassionate . . . merely because . . . you turn your head to look at Him.   (WP 26:5)

Communing like this with Jesus at prayer is again rooted in what Teresa has called 'an intimate sharing between friends' (*Life* 8:5).

In the inner room of the heart

We have already spoken of entering the 'inner room' of the heart, where we can commune with God 'in secret' (cf. Matt. 6.6). This is absolutely essential for the prayer of recollection, that gathering together of all one's faculties so as to focus exclusively on the presence of God. It implies the need to withdraw from externals that dissipate the energies – in prayer, that is, for it is not a call to neglect daily life – or, in Gospel terms, to 'shut the door' on all unnecessary distractions and idle wanderings of the mind (cf. Matt. 6.6). This is how Teresa describes this form of prayer:

> This prayer is called 'recollection', because the soul collects its faculties together and enters within itself to be with its God.   (WP 28:4)

Teresa assures us that this way of prayer is well suited to those 'who cannot engage in much discursive reflection with the intellect or keep [the] mind from distraction' (WP 26:2) – a description that probably applies to most people at one time or another. And she gives these encouraging words:

> Do you think it matters little for a soul with a wandering mind to . . .
> see that there is no need to go to heaven in order to speak with one's
> Eternal Father or find delight in Him? Nor is there any need to shout.
> However softly we speak, He is near enough to hear us. Neither is
> there any need for wings to go to find Him. All one need do is go into
> solitude and look at Him within oneself . . .   (WP 28:2)

Even more encouraging is that recollection is not a special grace
given to only a few. It is actually something we can *all* practise. To
quote Teresa: 'this recollection is . . . something we can desire and
achieve ourselves with the help of God' (WP 29:4). But while no
special grace is required for the practice of recollection, it stands at
the threshold of the higher forms of prayer – and, indeed, makes
them possible. It disposes us for a contemplative gaze – a gaze of faith
under the impulse of love[6] – and when we gaze on Christ, we open
ourselves to the graces he gives us in return, as and when he chooses
to do so: transforming us into his likeness, filling us with his life. To
gaze on Christ is to open up, as it were, a direct channel between
Jesus and ourselves. When God is at work in us, there are no limits
to what he can do, for 'nothing is impossible to God' (Luke 1.37).

Yes, in prayer God not only transforms the person who prays: 'It is
grace upon grace' (HL, p. 6), writes Edith Stein. It also prepares the
person to carry out a ministry for others, of which we see numerous
examples in Scripture: 'Saul awaited in solitary prayer the Lord's
answer to his question, "What do you want me to do?" In solitary
prayer Peter was prepared for his mission to the Gentiles' (HL, p. 13).
And prayer itself is mission and a force for good, to quote Edith once
more, reminding us here of the powerful impact of the prayer of each
one of us: 'Certainly the decisive turning points in world history are
substantially co-determined by souls whom no history book ever
mentions' (HL, p. 110).

And all this begins with that essential first step: the prayer of
recollection.

A tradition of Teresian prayer

While Teresa's teaching on prayer marks a high-point in the long
tradition of contemplative prayer, it does not signal the end. Several
other outstanding Carmelites continue the tradition as faithful
teacher-witnesses to Teresian prayer, each with their own original

touch and complementary teaching. These, too, can help us on our Lenten journey to enter, with loving eyes fixed on Jesus, deep into the desert of our own heart, to pray there in the spirit of the Gospels.

We have seen how the word of God permeates the Carmelite charism. This is just as true of Teresa and the other Carmelite saints. Each one of them is a unique embodiment of the spirit of Carmel, living and expressing it in their own original way. But for all their differences of time and culture, age and temperament, essentially they convey a common teaching on prayer, one that is deeply embedded in the Scriptures and especially the Gospels.

An inflow of God

St John of the Cross (1542–91) holds a special place in the Teresian charism. He was a close collaborator of Teresa – indeed, her co-founder – and she called him the 'father of [her] soul'. John, in particular, is known for laying out the map of the spiritual journey, and his writings on silent, contemplative prayer are inspirational. He stresses the *reality of God's indwelling in us* at the deepest centre of our being, where anyone can open themselves to the life of prayer:

> Since you know now that your desired Beloved lives hidden within your heart, strive to be really hidden with him, and you will embrace him within you and experience him with loving affection.   (SC 1:10)

And John penetrates for us into the *reality of what happens* as we open ourselves to God's action. In this memorable passage, already quoted, he writes:

> contemplation is nothing else than a secret and peaceful and loving inflow of God, which, if not hampered, fires the soul in the spirit of love . . .   (1DN 10:6)

As seen before, John also tells us that 'pure contemplation lies in receiving' (LF 3:36). Our part is to make ourselves capable of receiving and to increase our focus on God through detachment from all 'mental clutter', to use a modern expression: all that stands in the way of ('hampers', as above) this relationship. This requires a certain discipline or 'asceticism', on which the first book of *The Ascent of Mount Carmel* is excellent, which makes John particularly relevant as a guide for Lent.

An aspiration of the heart

St Thérèse of Lisieux (1873–97), the most recent Carmelite Doctor of the Church, might herself be called 'a word of God'. Her spirituality is rooted firmly in the Gospels and proclaims a Jesus who is nothing but love and mercy – in contrast to the prevailing climate of Jansenistic scruples and fear of God's justice. It is the gospel that was canonized today, commented, significantly, one priest in St Peter's Square, when the 'greatest saint of modern times' had just been raised to the altars.

Thérèse translates Teresian prayer for us into words that echo closely, and with her own original touch, Teresa's description of prayer as 'an intimate sharing between friends' (*Life* 8:5): 'I think that the Heart of my Spouse is mine alone, just as mine is His alone, and I speak to Him then in the solitude of this delightful heart to heart, while waiting to contemplate Him one day face to face . . .' (LT 122; r.e.). It is an intimate communion of love in total surrender to the love of Jesus. It already anticipates, here and now, the life of eternity.

Thérèse herself has penned a now famous description of prayer – part of which forms the introduction to prayer in the *Catechism of the Catholic Church* (§ 2558):

> For me, *prayer* is an aspiration of the heart, it is a simple glance directed to heaven, it is a cry of gratitude and love in the midst of trial as well as joy; finally, it is something great, supernatural, which expands my soul and unites me to Jesus. (SS, p. 242)

Such prayer itself unites her to Jesus who 'raised his eyes to heaven' (John 17.1), communing with his Father in a cry of gratitude and love, both at times of joy when he 'rejoiced in the Holy Spirit' (Luke 10.21) and in times of trial when he called out 'Abba, Father . . . remove this cup from me' (Mark 14.36), 'Save me from this hour' (John 12.27).

The suffering of Jesus, and its role in the spiritual life of Thérèse, makes her, like John of the Cross, an invaluable guide for Lent. Just as Teresa, in prayer, kept Jesus company when he was afflicted and alone (cf. *Life* 9:4), so Thérèse related to the vulnerable, eminently approachable Jesus – his 'heart burning with tenderness, . . . my brother . . . able to suffer' (PN 23:4). She communed with him through the words of Scripture: the hymn to the Suffering Servant in the prophet Isaiah (Isa. 52.13—53.12), which Thérèse described as 'the foundation' of her spirituality (LC, p. 135).

A little inner sanctuary

Forming a marvellous diptych, as it were, with Thérèse is her close contemporary, St Elizabeth of the Trinity (1880–1906), who also draws considerable inspiration from the New Testament. With her unerring depth of insight, Elizabeth shares with us her message of 'heaven on earth', which is one of her greatest hallmarks:

> We possess our Heaven within us, since He who satisfies the hunger of the glorified in the light of vision gives Himself to us in faith and mystery, it is the Same One! It seems to me that I have found my Heaven on earth, since Heaven is God, and God is [in] my soul. The day I understood that, everything became clear to me.   (L 122)

Heaven is where God is. And God – Father, Son and Holy Spirit – is in the heart of all believers. This is what we are invited to take to heart when Jesus says to us of himself and his Father: 'we will come to them and make our home in them' (John 14.23) – one of Elizabeth's favourite lines from the Gospels. This profound mystery of the indwelling of the Trinity is central to Elizabeth's teaching on prayer, just as it is the foundation on which Teresa of Avila builds the inner journey of prayer towards the centre of the soul – 'this little heaven of our soul, where [Jesus] dwells' (WP 28:5), she wrote, in a phrase that would delight Elizabeth. It was a 'secret' Elizabeth wanted to 'whisper' to others, as she put it, 'so they too might always cling to God through everything' (L 122).

A Jacob's ladder

One of the more recent Carmelite saints is Edith Stein (1891–1942), martyred at Auschwitz. She invites us to a silent listening to the word of God as the source of all fruitful activity in the Church: 'We need hours for listening silently and allowing the Word of God to act on us,' she writes, 'until it moves us to bear fruit in an offering of praise and an offering of action' (HL, p. 16). A Gospel image comes readily to mind here: that of Martha's sister, Mary, who 'has chosen the better part' (Luke 10.42), sitting at the feet of Jesus and listening to his word. The quotation from Edith recalls, too, these words of Jesus: 'Blessed are those who hear the word of God and *do* it' (Luke 11.28).

Edith also gives us some good advice on how to listen silently. It is both helpful and simple, and captures perfectly the 'inner room' spoken of by Jesus and Teresa's description of prayer as 'an intimate sharing between friends':

> The only essential is that one finds, first of all, a quiet corner in which one can communicate with God as though there were nothing else, and that must be done daily. (SP, p. 54)

All Edith's greatness as a writer and lecturer, philosopher and feminist, is peripheral to – but also the fruit of – her deep inner life of silent listening to the word in prayer. She herself assures us: 'Prayer is the highest achievement of which the human spirit is capable' (HL, p. 38).

As a Jewish woman steeped in the Hebrew Scriptures, Edith Stein is a bridge between the Old Testament and the New, and this may well be her most original contribution to the mystery of Christian prayer. She draws, for example, a telling image of prayer from Genesis: 'Prayer is a Jacob's ladder on which the human spirit ascends to God and God's grace descends to people' (HL, p. 38). But perhaps most central of all to her spirituality is her understanding of the passion of Jesus in the light of the 'Day of Atonement', the Jewish holy day of 'Yom Kippur', which she rightly refers to as 'the Old Testament antecedent of Good Friday' (HL, p. 12). This was when the high priest, once a year, entered the Holy of Holies in the Jerusalem Temple, to offer sacrifice for the sins of himself and all the people. To meditate on this highest sacrifice in the Jewish Temple, as described in Leviticus 16, alongside the Gospel accounts of the passion of Jesus, gives us abundant spiritual food for Lent. Edith also highlights the often overlooked links between the prayer of the high priest (cf. Lev. 16.17; 1 Kings 8.52, 41–43) and the priestly prayer of Jesus (John 17.1–26). This prayer in John, so loved by the Carmelite saints, provides our final reflection in this chapter.

Carmel and the priestly prayer

There is a long Carmelite tradition nourished and inspired by the priestly prayer of Jesus. Teresa refers to this long and moving prayer when she describes the highest form of the mystical life. She calls it a 'mirror that we contemplate, where our image is engraved' (IC VII:2:8): that is, a mirror in which the soul which has reached the highest peaks can see itself reflected; a mirror in which the soul sees itself at one with the highest prayer of Jesus as he holds all believers before the face of the Father.

We are told that on his journeys John of the Cross constantly repeated, quietly and with great devotion, this same priestly prayer. Revealingly, in his teaching John was at a loss for words to explain the mystery of final transforming union – even allowing for the lines of his incomparable lyric poetry: 'the breathing of the air... / in the serene night, / with a flame that is consuming and painless' (SC, stanza 39). Then he found the answer: to convey the highest union with God, he simply quoted verse after verse of the priestly prayer (cf. SC 39:5).

Elizabeth of the Trinity – alert to sharing in the life of eternity, here and now – several times in her writings recalls verses of the priestly prayer, even some verses again and again (John 17.4, 19, 21). She reminds her sister: '[Jesus] wills that where He is we should be also, not only for eternity, but already in time' (HF 1; cf. John 17.24). And the reason she wishes that everyone might 'cling to God through everything' is so that 'this prayer of Christ might be fulfilled: "Father, may they be made perfectly one!"' (L 122; cf. John 17.23).

Thérèse, just before her death, emulating Jesus before his own passing from this life, chooses to speak to God in the words of the priestly prayer, which she repeats at great length, like John of the Cross (cf. SS, p. 255). It is like her dying gasp, a prelude to her prayer of promised intercession for others throughout eternity.

For Edith Stein, the priestly prayer is the ultimate fulfilment of the intimate exchange of the high priest with God in the secret, innermost part of the Temple, and the ultimate revelation of the communion between God the Father and Jesus, our high priest, 'in the Holy of Holies of his heart' (HL, p. 12). Inviting us to ponder John 17 and to learn how to pray as Jesus did, she writes:

> he unlocks the mystery of the high priest's realm. All who belong to
> him may hear how, in the Holy of Holies of his heart, he speaks to his
> Father; they are to experience what is going on and are to learn to
> speak to the Father in their own hearts.   (HL, p. 12)

The one who does this perfectly, Edith shows us, is the mother of Jesus: for Mary, 'who kept every word sent from God in her heart, is the model for such attentive souls in whom Jesus' high priestly prayer comes to life again and again' (HL, p. 13).

Teresa, John of the Cross, Thérèse, Elizabeth, Edith Stein, and many other Carmelite women and men of prayer – all these rank among those 'attentive souls'. In them the priestly prayer lives on, embedded in the Carmelite tradition of Teresian prayer.

————◆————

Questions for reflection or discussion

1 Think of how you relate to your best friend and how this can help you in your relationship with Jesus who is your Friend.

2 Does any one of the Carmelite saints speak to you more power-fully than the others, and why?

3 What are the ways in which Carmelite prayer can be life-changing?

5

His heart an open wound
The love that leads to Calvary

———◆◆◆———

We travel on our Lenten journey as weak, broken, wounded, sinful members of a fragile Church. We carry with us the burden of our failures, vulnerability, powerlessness, even despair, and moments of apparent abandonment by God. Lent is a challenge for all of us to walk in the truth about ourselves and about God: to journey with Jesus as our Companion throughout life, and especially the most challenging times in our life. Jesus can show us the truth of our own weakness, insecurity and brokenness, but at the same time he reveals to us the truth of a God who is mercy, compassion and tenderness, as we see from this remarkable passage in the Letter to the Hebrews:

> [Jesus] is able to sympathise with our weaknesses, one who in every way has been tempted as we are, yet without sinning . . . he can deal gently with the ignorant and wayward, since he himself is beset with weakness. (Heb. 4.15; 5.2)

This is a Jesus who can speak to our anxious, confused and troubled world – a world that searches for meaning and purpose; that wrestles with the problem of pain, especially innocent suffering; that sees death as meaningless; that is unable to believe in the existence of God, let alone in his love and compassion for each of us personally. This encouraging message of God's merciful love is found again and again in the teaching of the Carmelite saints. They speak of a Jesus who is himself weak, broken, fragile, humble of heart, who even knew what it was to feel abandoned by God. Carmel stresses this incredible truth: *that the all-powerful God is in need of our love.*

'Beset with weakness'

This is, without doubt, one of the most human and appealing aspects of Teresian spirituality. It can also be life-changing when one embraces the truth of a Jesus who is weak and vulnerable – who is so very understanding and approachable. For Teresa, this human face of Jesus led her to discover a God happy to take on our lowly nature, which is why he is both accessible and compassionate:

> Christ is a very good friend because we behold Him as man and see Him with weaknesses and trials . . . I saw that He was man, even though He was God; that He wasn't surprised by human weaknesses; that He understands our miserable make-up, subject to many falls . . . I can speak with Him as with a friend, even though He is Lord.
>
> (*Life* 22:10; 37:5)

This self-lowering or 'self-emptying' of Jesus, which reaches its climax in the passion, was in fact a constant in his life: 'he emptied himself, taking the condition of a slave' (Phil. 2.7). This never ceased to touch Teresa deeply: 'He came from the bosom of His Father out of obedience to become our slave' (F 5:17), she tells us. So she reminds us that we are 'useless servants' (Luke 17.10), fortunate 'to be able to repay [God] something of what we owe Him for His service toward us'. And she comments: 'I say these words "His service toward us" unwillingly; but the fact is that He did nothing else but serve us all the time He lived in this world' (IC III:1:8); 'it seems that Jesus is honoured to be [a slave]' (WP 33:4).

To emulate Jesus in this way is to respond like St Thérèse of Lisieux. Perhaps more than anyone, Thérèse embraced her own frailty and powerlessness, for they provided her with the whole foundation of her teaching on the mercy of God, who lifts up and carries the 'little ones' who have confidence in him. Thérèse also has a great need for love. And the face of Jesus in the Gospels fulfilled all her needs: for there, she discovered a Jesus weak and vulnerable like herself – and, like herself, in need of love. She cried out:

> I need a heart burning with tenderness,
> Who will be my support forever,
> Who loves everything in me, even my weakness . . .
> And who never leaves me day or night.
> I could find no creature
> Who could always love me and never die.

I must have a God who takes on my nature
And becomes my brother and is able to suffer!
(PN 23:4; r.e.)

This is the lesson that Thérèse, like Teresa, found embodied in the person of Jesus: he can deal gently with the weak and the wayward because he himself is meek and humble of heart. But more than this: with her own original slant, Thérèse could see that the self-lowering of Jesus holds the great potential for us to *be transformed in God through union with him.*

Thérèse knew, at first hand, what it was to be transformed. We do her no favours if we think that she was always a saint. Her mother said of the young Thérèse: 'one doesn't know how things will go . . . she is . . . so thoughtless . . . and has a stubborn streak in her that is almost invincible' (SS, p. 22). And she was sensitive, touchy, moody. Then, when she was only four, her mother died, and the happy, carefree Thérèse became timid and scrupulous, easily dissolving into tears.

Almost ten years later, returning from Midnight Mass that Christmas, Thérèse was about to burst into tears yet again, when she found herself suddenly strengthened. In an instant, God had helped her to grow up and restored her happy character. Thérèse describes this as the fruit of union with God: for at Mass, she said, she had 'had the happiness of receiving the *strong* and *powerful* God' (SS, p. 98).

In Carmel, Thérèse would write of transformation in this striking way (referring here to God as 'Love'): 'Yes, in order that Love be fully satisfied, it is necessary that It lower Itself, and that It lower Itself to nothingness and transform this nothingness into *fire*' (SS, p. 195). No wonder she could rejoice in her 'nothingness' and describe it as the greatest grace of her life: 'I prefer to agree very simply that the Almighty has done great things [in me] . . . and the greatest thing is to have shown [me my] *littleness*, [my] powerlessness' (SS, p. 210; cf. Luke 1.49). We see, here, the love for Jesus that engenders humility.

Walking in the truth

Teresa speaks of humility as 'truth': 'to be humble is to walk in truth, for it is a very deep truth that of ourselves we have nothing good [in us]' (IC VI:10:7). For Teresa, a large part of 'walking in truth' is self-knowledge – knowing ourselves to be mere creatures, weak and flawed. She writes: 'I consider one day of humble self-knowledge a greater favour from the Lord, even though the day may have cost us numerous afflictions and trials, than many days of prayer' (F 5:16; cf. IC III:1:9).

Thérèse, too, links humility and truth. Right at the end of her life, on her last day on earth, she could say: 'I never sought anything but the truth; yes, I have understood humility of heart . . . It seems to me I'm humble' (LC, p. 205; r.e.). What this reveals is Thérèse's long-standing and constant striving to emulate Jesus. He is the exemplar of all the virtues, but humility is a virtue he explicitly asks us to learn *by following his example*: 'Learn of me,' he says, 'for I am meek and humble of heart' (Matt. 11.29). This link between meekness and humility is significant: it shows us Jesus describing himself as gentle and sensitive.

Repeatedly, Jesus affirms the important lesson of humility. We see this, for example, in the parable of the Pharisee and the tax-collector (a public sinner or 'publican') in the Temple: 'all who exalt themselves will be humbled,' he says, 'but those who humble themselves will be exalted' (Luke 18.14; cf. 14.11; Matt. 18.4; 23.12). Unlike the Pharisee, the public sinner walked the way of truth: the truth of his own *weakness* and *insecurity*, his own misery and sinfulness – and the truth of a God who is *mercy*, *compassion* and *tenderness*. In a word: a God of love!

This is the God of truth – and the truth of God – whom Thérèse, a true daughter of Teresa, discovered in the Gospels: the God before whom she rejoiced to be *small* and *lowly* and *vulnerable*, dependent on his mercy. The important thing about the reaction of the saints – *all* the saints, not only the saints of Carmel – is that their focus is not on themselves so much as on God. To know oneself sinful is to *focus most of all on God's mercy*. Thérèse, who is actually known as the 'Doctor of Merciful Love', did this to an outstanding degree, as we see from the last words she ever wrote in her *Story of a Soul*, which are about this very parable:

> I don't hasten to the first place but to the last; rather than advance like the Pharisee, I repeat, filled with confidence, the publican's humble prayer . . . Yes, I feel it; even though I had on my conscience all the sins that can be committed, I would go, my heart broken with sorrow,

and throw myself into Jesus' arms . . . I go to Him with confidence and
love . . .   (SS, pp. 258–9; r.e. at end)

Unrequited love

Jesus had once revealed himself to Teresa as a 'living book' (*Life* 26:5), and it was in this very 'book' that Teresa read the story of God's 'self-emptying' in the passion of his Son. Teresa was not a born saint: she had to pass through a number of 'conversions' before her so-called 'final conversion'. She would say of her early years: 'so hard was my heart that I could read the entire Passion without shedding a tear' (*Life* 3:1). But in 1554, after nearly twenty years in Carmel, all that changed.

One day, entering the convent oratory, she was praying before an *Ecce Homo* statue of Jesus, when the sight of the 'much wounded Christ' – blood-stained and helpless – evoked in her 'what He suffered for us'. This happened in such a vivid and lifelike way that 'it seems to me,' she said, 'my heart broke' (*Life* 9:1).

This life-changing experience was to mark a great turning-point in Teresa's life, and the nature of it has had a strong influence on the Teresian charism to this day. The fruit of this experience brings us to another of the more human and appealing aspects of Teresian spirituality – a dimension of God that is so easily overlooked: his *unrequited love*. Its pinnacle is the passion of Jesus, for here we reach the summit of God's love, rejected and disdained: 'God so loved the world that he gave his only Son' (John 3.16), we read in the Gospel of John, who also tells us that 'his own did not accept him' (John 1.11).

A most moving expression of this is a simple and beautiful poem by John of the Cross, who invites us to reflect on the pain of this unrequited love in the heart of Jesus on the cross. 'The Little Shepherd Boy' (P 7) is a love poem, a romance, with a haunting refrain: '*his heart an open wound with love*'. It depicts Jesus as a young shepherd in love with a shepherdess who symbolizes each one of us. Indeed, she is the whole Church, loved by God with an everlasting love – even when he is not loved in return. Notably, the 'shepherdess' embodies our reluctance – our frequent reluctance – to respond to Jesus with love for love. Much of the content of these verses has been adapted by John from a popular ballad of his day. But to these the saint significantly adds a final stanza, on the radical demands of sacrificial love, crucified love, God's gift of himself to each of us and to the Church. It is a pure, self-giving and forgiving love.

If we ponder the message of this final stanza, it will invite us to search deep into our own hearts, into every dark and hidden crevice, so as to be no longer the heartless shepherdess who brings him only pain:

> After a long time he climbed a tree,
> and spread his beautiful arms,
> and hung by them, and died,
> *his heart an open wound with love.*
>
> (P 7:5)

A pierced heart on fire with love

We can only marvel at John's vision in this climax to his poem. Gazing on the crucified Christ, he sees this heart-rending image of beautiful arms outstretched to save a world that rejects him. Of all John's writings, this must surely rank among his most moving lines. It is a heartfelt and honest response to the biblical call to 'look on him whom they have pierced' (John 19.37; cf. Zech. 12.10). Even more than the wounded limbs, it is the *pierced heart* of Christ that John of the Cross sees. And this heart calls for *a response of love*.

That is what prayer is, in the Teresian tradition, which is why the truth of God's unrequited love appeals in a special way to Carmelites, called by vocation to a life of prayer; 'do not withdraw from the cross or abandon it,' Teresa tells us, '... Fix your eyes on the Crucified and everything will become small for you ...' – words faithfully echoed by her Carmelite daughter Elizabeth of the Trinity: 'Take your Crucifix, look, listen' (WP 26:7; IC VII:4:8; L 93). If we do no more than this in our Lenten prayer, we will have done everything. And when we look – what will we see? When we listen – what will we hear? It is worth pondering this for a while. The answers that come to us may be different from what we expect. The message of Christian salvation is that Jesus died on a cross to save all people and give us eternal life. No Carmelite would disagree with this: it is the central truth of our faith. But there is a difference of emphasis in our Carmelite tradition.

Edith Stein, like the other Carmelite saints, invites us to keep our eyes fixed on the Crucified. And there, she sees how much *he wants us to give him our love*. She does not tell us that Christ died to save us

– a truth of faith which she was not, of course, questioning. Rather, she highlights this spiritual aspect, for us to take to heart:

> The arms of the Crucified are spread out to draw you to his heart. He wants your life in order to give you his. (HL, p. 95)

It is, once more, the little shepherd boy of John of the Cross; the *Ecce Homo* figure of Teresa's conversion; 'if anyone is seeking God,' says John, 'the Beloved is seeking that person much more' (LF 3:28).

The maternal heart of God

In her own original way, Thérèse captures beautifully this aspect of the Carmelite charism. It is no exaggeration to say that it set her heart on fire. Reflecting on the Gospels revealed to her God's unrequited love, and she wants to draw our attention to this urgently. She expresses it in terms of *prayer as a response to love*:

> On every side this love is unknown, rejected . . . Is Your disdained Love going to remain closed up within Your Heart? (SS, pp. 180–1)

Two years before her death, Thérèse offers her life to the God of mercy, in a document which is known as her *Act of Oblation to Merciful Love*. This now classic prayer ends with her painful cry of love to God, asking him to allow 'the waves of *infinite tenderness* shut up within You to overflow into my soul' (SS, p. 277).

From a young age, Thérèse had been profoundly struck by the cry of Jesus on the cross, '*I thirst!*' (SS, p. 99; John 19.28). This 'thirst', she saw, was *a thirst for love*. It is prefigured in the episode of the Samaritan woman where Jesus is reaching out for love when he asks her for water: 'Give me to drink' (John 4.7). Or, to quote Thérèse: 'it was the *love* of His poor creature the Creator of the universe was seeking. He was thirsty for love' (SS, p. 189). If we could only see in the light of truth, *we* would be thirsty for *his* love. 'If you knew the gift of God . . .' (John 4.10), Jesus also says to the Samaritan woman, a line that always thrilled Elizabeth of the Trinity.

This love of Jesus has all the feminine qualities of a caring mother's tender love: patience, understanding, readiness always to forgive. In Isaiah, Thérèse read with joy that God cares for us like a mother (cf. Isa. 66.12–13). And it was in Jesus that she, who lost her mother at the age of four, discovered the maternal heart of God: eternal, merciful love shining through human weakness and thirsting for her own love in return. She says: 'I felt at the bottom of my heart that . . . God is more tender than a mother' (SS, p. 174).

Love crucified

Edith Stein, a Jewish woman and Carmelite saint, was also a brilliant philosopher. By definition, then, she was a 'lover of wisdom'. At fifteen, she became an atheist – or at the very least, an agnostic – and at the same time she decided to give up praying. But she never lost her longing for truth. Much later, after her conversion, she would look back on those years of unbelief and feel able to say: 'My longing for truth was a prayer in itself.'[1] But what, for Edith, was 'truth'?

Edith first discovered the mystery of the cross when she was still an agnostic. In 1917, a good friend of hers, the philosopher Adolf Reinach, died in combat. He and his wife were Lutherans, converts from Judaism. Wondering how she could possibly comfort the young widow, Edith observed in amazement how Anne had accepted the pain of her husband's death. And in a flash of enlightenment, Edith saw her to be at one with Christ's suffering. This marked an important breakthrough in Edith's understanding of Jesus as the promised Messiah. She would recount it years later, as vividly as if it had only just happened:

> It was then that I first encountered the Cross and the divine strength which it inspires in those who bear it. For the first time I saw before my very eyes the Church, born of Christ's redemptive suffering, victorious over the sting of death. It was the moment in which my unbelief was shattered, Judaism paled, and Christ streamed out upon me: Christ in the mystery of the Cross.[2]

This philosopher's search had led her to the crucified Christ, described by Paul as 'the power of God and the wisdom of God' (1 Cor. 1.24). Here was a face of God which, until then, had been unknown to Edith as a Jewish woman: *a suffering Messiah*. It impelled her to follow Christ by helping him carry his cross, and it revealed this to her as the special vocation of the Christian. She would write:

> The Saviour is not alone on the way of the cross . . . The lovers of the cross whom he has awakened and will always continue to awaken anew

in the changeable history of the struggling church, these are his allies at the end of time. We, too, are called for that purpose.   (HL, p. 92)

Lovers of the cross

This powerful quotation comes from an essay which Edith entitled 'Love of the Cross' (cf. HL, pp. 91–3). Despite the challenging nature of this expression – something not humanly possible without God's grace – the faithful daughters and sons of Teresa are, like Teresa herself, true lovers of the wisdom of the cross. Each of the saints we are considering here travelled, by way of their own painful experiences, in the wake of the Suffering Servant.

Thérèse of Lisieux entered deeply through the Servant Song of Isaiah (cf. Isa. 52.13—53.12) into the mystery of suffering.[3] There, she discovered the love that is both hidden and revealed in human weakness. Her own father had always radiated for her the beauty of God's love. But now, suddenly stricken with mental illness, he was beset with anguish and looked a mere semblance of his former self. At this time, Thérèse confided to her sister Pauline:

> These words of Isaiah [from the Song of the Suffering Servant] . . . have made the whole foundation of my devotion to the Holy Face, or, to express it better, the foundation of all my piety.   (LC, p. 135)

Thérèse would now contemplate Jesus, the suffering Messiah, his radiant face distorted by pain, like a beautiful object reflected on rippling water. It was this image of a suffering God that opened up for her the mystery of God's love. It inspired her to try and remove all the layers of selfishness in herself, and to give herself totally to God for others. She expresses this divesting of herself with a simple image: it is, she says, like unpetalling a rose (cf. PN 51). This expression may at first sight appear childish and sentimental. But the reality of which it speaks is a total and absolute self-giving in response to love, revealed in what Thérèse calls 'the HIDDEN BEAUTIES of Jesus' (LT 108) – Jesus as the Suffering Servant. We could apply to him these remarkable words of the poet Patrick Kavanagh: 'Maybe this's what he was born for, this hour / Of hopelessness.'[4]

The Jesus whom Thérèse found in the Gospels was the Word-made-weakness: 'a God who . . . is able to suffer' (PN 23:4), she wrote, and she needed this Jesus, with whom she could identify fully. For he was, quite simply, human. The Jesus of Thérèse 'sweated blood' (cf. Luke 22.44), 'offered up prayers and supplications, with loud cries and tears' (Heb. 5.7), and on the way to Calvary he stumbled and fell – again and again and again. This is what makes Thérèse remarkably original in her approach to suffering. She assures us that we do not have to suffer heroically, or even courageously. The worst kind of suffering, she tells us, is not being able to suffer *well*. However, by 'well' she does not mean heroically, as we might at first think. Rather, she makes this surprising statement: 'What an unspeakable joy to carry our Crosses FEEBLY' (LT 82). And in another letter to her sister Céline:

> Let us suffer the bitter pain, without courage! . . . (Jesus suffered in *sadness*! Without sadness would the soul suffer! . . .) And still we would like to suffer generously, grandly! . . . Céline! what an illusion! . . . We'd never want to fall? . . . What does it matter, my Jesus, if I fall at each moment; *I see* my weakness through this and this is a great gain for me . . .   (LT 89; r.e.)

Thérèse, though, teaches us to do much more than just accept passively the inevitable pain of the human condition. She invites us to turn it into a way of loving. Every kind of human suffering – fear, anguish, loneliness, depression, even dying itself, can be transfigured by trust and love. We cannot choose to suffer or not to suffer, to die or not to die. It is all part of the human condition. But we can choose to love or not to love. Suffering can make monsters of some and saints of others. It's all in the attitude.

Contemplating the Crucified

For Elizabeth of the Trinity, as for Thérèse, God's love was inseparable from the passion of Jesus. Elizabeth longed in particular to be transformed into Christ crucified, as in these words of St Paul that she loved so much: 'to share in his sufferings, reproducing the pattern of his death' (Phil. 3.10; cf. HF 28). Another of her favourite passages from St Paul captures perfectly the abiding disposition of her heart:

> With Christ I hang upon the cross, and yet I am alive; or rather, not I; it is Christ that lives in me. True, I am living, here and now, this mortal life; but my real life is the faith I have in the Son of God, who loved me, and delivered himself up for me. (Gal. 2.20; cf. L 214; LR 13; GV 11)

In her famous *Prayer to the Trinity*, Elizabeth distils into a few lines the essence of her response to Love Crucified:

> O my beloved Christ, crucified by love . . . I wish to love You . . . even unto death! But I feel my weakness, and I ask You to 'clothe me with Yourself' . . . that I may be another humanity for [You] in which [You] can renew [Your] whole Mystery.
>
> (PT; r.e. second instance; cf. Gal. 3.27)

To be 'another humanity' for Christ speaks of Elizabeth's offering herself to God's 'creative Action', as she expresses it in the same prayer, so that she might, like St Paul, be able to say: 'it is Christ that lives in me' (Gal. 2.20). And she sums up her Carmelite vocation – and its fruitfulness for the whole Church – as a calling to live at one with Christ crucified. Elizabeth also realized that to do this, we need to *contemplate* Jesus in his passion, for *we resemble the model we contemplate*. To look and listen before the cross of Christ will soon lead to wanting to do what he did.

We noted earlier how God's unrequited love calls for a response of love. This is expressed in our prayer and in our Christian works. It is also the key to uniting contemplation and action: they often seem like separate activities, difficult to combine; but any such difference is banished when they are seen in the light of a response to the heart of God. Elizabeth of the Trinity, contemplating the cross of Christ, expresses this beautifully, and also highlights the fact that this response to God's love is an imitation of Christ. She writes:

> A Carmelite . . . is a soul who has *gazed on the Crucified*, who has seen Him offering Himself to His Father as a Victim for souls and, recollecting herself in this great vision of the charity of Christ, has understood the passionate love of His soul, and has wanted to give herself as He did! (L 133)

However weak and vulnerable she felt herself to be, she knew she was united with Christ and that her suffering was fruitful. This conviction makes all the difference: one can suffer in frustration and despair, or else one can know joy (which can actually exist alongside pain). So, like Paul she could say: 'I rejoice in my sufferings . . .' (Col. 1.24; cf. GV 7). These were not mere words or pious wishful thinking. Others attest to her unwavering joy even as she was dying: 'lovable and engaging even during the most acute sufferings of her last days . . .

Her smile never left her lips . . . very forgetful of her own sufferings.'[5] We could sum up her disposition no better than with her own words: 'a soul united to Jesus is a living smile that radiates Him and gives Him!' (L 252). In her, grace was the hidden smile of her soul.

Wisdom through the cross

John of the Cross was no stranger to deep suffering; and few, if any, have entered more deeply into the mystery of God's love concealed and revealed in the wisdom of the cross. It is significant that after he has spoken of the heights of holiness, near the end of his *Spiritual Canticle*, he pauses to share with us his mature insights into the value of pain and suffering in God's loving plan of salvation. He speaks of entering 'further, deep into the thicket' (SC, stanza 36), which he explains in this way:

> Oh! If we could but now fully understand how a soul cannot reach the thicket and wisdom of the riches of God, which are of many kinds, without entering the thicket of many kinds of suffering, finding in this her delight and consolation; and how a soul with an authentic desire for divine wisdom wants suffering first in order to enter this wisdom by the thicket of the cross! . . . The gate entering into these riches of his wisdom is the cross . . . (SC 36:13)

John goes on to speak of 'the high caverns in the rock / that are so well concealed' (SC, stanza 37). He explains that the 'rock', referred to here, 'as St Paul says, is Christ' (cf. 1 Cor. 10.4), and that the 'high caverns' of this rock are 'the sublime, exalted, and deep mysteries of God's wisdom in Christ' (SC 37:3); he further adds that they are 'so well concealed' because there is 'much to fathom in Christ' (SC 37:4) – and John describes him here as a deep mine of hidden treasures. But, he remarks: 'The soul cannot enter these caverns or reach these treasures if, as we said, she does not first pass over to the divine wisdom through the straits of exterior and interior suffering' (SC 37:4).

Such remarks, however, can be seen as misleading or even frightening. They might appear to suggest that anyone who wishes to become holy will then be subject to sufferings of every kind. This sounds so daunting that people might be tempted to settle for a lukewarm spiritual life instead. Rather, there are two important points to remember.

One is that suffering is an inevitable part of the human condition: *no human being is exempt*. The question, then, is: how should we respond in the face of our sufferings, or rather how does God wish us to respond? So, John's words should be seen as an invitation to unite our *already existing* sufferings with those of Christ (something which, through this union with him in prayer, can, paradoxically, make them more bearable!); and to realize, consolingly, that our sufferings are working in us powerfully to fashion us in the likeness of Christ, and to build up the body of Christ, as Paul writes in Colossians: 'I rejoice in my sufferings for your sake, and in my flesh I complete what is lacking in Christ's sufferings for the sake of his body, that is, the church' (Col. 1.24).

The second thing to note is that every trial or suffering is accompanied by a special grace of God – *at the time: not in advance* – to help us carry this cross. As spiritual people often attest from personal experience: 'God does not give us more sufferings than he will help us to bear.' Or, to quote another powerful passage from St Paul: '[The Lord] said to me, "My grace is sufficient for you, for my power is made perfect in weakness." I will all the more gladly boast of my weaknesses, that the power of Christ may rest upon me' (2 Cor. 12.9).

Witnesses for today

What, though, of all the masses of people today who have no faith in Christ? All those who grapple anxiously with the mystery of suffering, especially innocent suffering; those who find no purpose in life, and for whom death itself is something dreaded and meaningless. Do the Carmelite saints, who found purpose in uniting their sufferings to those of Christ, have anything meaningful to say to our searching, doubting, troubled world? In *The Mystery of Christmas*, Edith Stein evokes the gentle picture of the stable at Bethlehem, where the followers of the Infant Jesus are drawn to come and be with him. Yet Edith's portrayal is no usual crib scene: for along with the shepherds and the Magi are those whom the Child Jesus has called to *take up their cross and give their lives for him*. There is John, the Beloved Disciple, who followed Jesus all the way to Golgotha. There is Stephen, who was killed as he witnessed to Christ. And, most surprisingly of all: the little ones whom we know as the 'Holy Innocents'.

These are the ones who *suffer for Christ without knowing him.* They have no ideals about offering their life for a higher cause, and yet in their innocent suffering they have become the followers of Christ. 'You children,' Edith says to them, 'who as yet cannot give of your own free will, of you these little hands [of the Child Jesus] will request your gentle life before it has even begun; it can serve no better purpose than sacrifice in praise of the Lord' (MC, p. 8). *All* suffering, then, endured willingly or not, whether we are conscious of its value or not, is a participation in Christ's redemptive work. In the end, this is a mystery – as deep and impenetrable as the paschal mystery itself. Only in heaven will it all become clear.

But we also have the remarkable witness of Thérèse, for those who struggle without faith in God. Thérèse does not preach to atheists, much less condemn them: she identifies fully with their pain and anguish; she reaches out to them; she embraces them as their companion in search of the 'Unknown God' (cf. Acts 17.23). She reveals to them the face of a God who is all mercy, tenderness, forgiveness; a God with a maternal heart who knows and loves them in their darkness and their struggle. She confesses that 'Jesus made me feel that there were really souls who have no faith' (SS, p. 211). These atheists are her 'brothers and sisters', she tells us. She shares with them and with us her long months of temptations against faith. Her thoughts were filled with the worst thoughts of the 'materialists'. She trod the brink of 'blasphemy' and recounts the voices mocking her previous serenity of faith:

> 'You are dreaming about the light, about a fatherland embalmed in the sweetest perfumes; you are dreaming about the *eternal* possession of the Creator of all these marvels; you believe that one day you will walk out of this fog that surrounds you! Advance, advance; rejoice in death which will give you not what you hope for but a night still more profound, the night of nothingness.'   (SS, p. 213)

Transformed into love

This brings us to a final reflection: on those times *when even believers suffer for Christ without, it seems to them, knowing him.* At times when all is darkness unrelieved. Physical suffering is never easy, although it usually helps greatly to keep our eyes fixed on Christ. But if he seems to be no longer there? Not hearing our prayer? Not even existing? This is a particular torment – a sign of the highest testing – and it goes all the way back to Christ himself when he cried out on the cross: 'My God, my God, why have you forsaken me?' (Matt. 27.46).

In the Carmelite tradition, suffering of this kind is perhaps best considered with regard to Thérèse, given her acute and harrowing trial of faith throughout the last eighteen months of her life. As with Jesus, her greatest trial of darkness occurred at the same time as her worst physical sufferings. Indeed, these were so bad that, near the end, she confessed that the pain was enough 'to make her lose her reason' (LC, p. 162; cf. 163 and 196), and she even felt tempted to suicide. Her trial of faith reached no less terrible a pitch.

She described this as the 'thickest darkness' (SS, p. 211) which had invaded her soul. No doubt the worst torture of all were her 'temptations against faith', the mocking voices, of which we have just spoken, proclaiming a 'night of nothingness' (SS, p. 213). But Thérèse continued to be faithful to Jesus with every fibre of her being. It matured her in ways she could not suspect at the time. But we get an insight into the work God was doing in her soul, when she made this confidence right in the midst of the darkness: 'it seems to me that after this mortal life there is nothing left . . . Everything has disappeared for me, love is all I have.'[6] And that 'love is all I have' is the sign that Thérèse was being transformed into God who is 'love' (cf. 1 John 4.16).

There *is* nothing more important than love. It leads us to love God with our whole being, and to love our neighbour even as Jesus did: to the point of 'laying down our life' for others (cf. John 15.13; 1 John 3.16). It was *love* that led Jesus to Calvary.

Questions for reflection or discussion

1 What image of Jesus draws you most easily to him? Do you live your life in imitation of this example and respond to him in this light?

2 What aspects of Carmelite teaching open up new dimensions for you of the person of Jesus?

3 How would your prayer be transformed if you fully took on board the reality of God's unrequited love?

6

Into all truth
Led by the Holy Spirit

———◆———

The Holy Spirit is often overlooked, during Lent, as we follow Jesus on his path to Calvary. But it is the Spirit who led Jesus into all his trials and who sustained him in them. We see this clearly from the very first trials in the Gospels: the temptations in the desert. Jesus had just received the Holy Spirit at baptism. Then, immediately he was 'led by the Spirit into the wilderness' (Matt. 4.1), where he did battle with the devil for forty days and nights, and emerged victorious – strengthened by the Holy Spirit and bearing witness to the Father with the word of God.

Carmel itself is traditionally thought of as a 'desert', and its charism is a desert spirituality. Our saints were impelled by the Holy Spirit to give themselves totally to God; they then entered the Carmelite desert of the monastery – but, still more so, of their heart; there, they had an intense encounter with the Lord, along with many temptations and trials – armed with prayer and the word of God.

The saints have always followed the example of Jesus, in this respect as in every other. We see St Paul, for example, who, after the momentous experience of his conversion, received the Holy Spirit (cf. Acts 9.17) and was then impelled to go into the desert (cf. Gal. 1.17) – after which, he emerged strengthened and began a ministry that would make him one of the founding fathers of the Church and shape the faith that is ours today.

This chapter will shed light on passages from the writings of the Carmelite saints, to show how they were *guided* by the Spirit in their daily lives and *enlightened* at the proper time, entered into the mystery of God whom the Spirit *revealed* to them, were inflamed with *desire for God*, opened themselves in prayer to God's work of *transformation*, and how in illness and in other trials they were *strengthened* by the Spirit and thereby *bore witness to Christ* – through the power of God that is the Holy Spirit.

'At the Spring of living waters'

The rest of this chapter will explore these questions. But by way of prelude to this discussion, we need always to bear in mind that, for the Carmelite saints, the Holy Spirit was always a Person, with whom they related. For Carmelite prayer is, most essentially, *relationship* with God – with the three Persons of the Trinity, each in their own way. And this relating is deeply contemplative, and involves an openness and surrender to the work of the Spirit.

A hallmark of the Carmelite saints, as mentioned before in this book, is the contemplative nature of their prayer. And this gazing on God, combined with deep faith, assures them that God is gazing at us, too, at every moment. To receive the Holy Spirit, then, is simply to expose the depth of our soul, without resistance, to his action, so that we may be transformed into the likeness of Christ. Elizabeth of the Trinity speaks eloquently of the need to be 'a soul of silence that remains like a lyre under the mysterious touch of the Holy Spirit so that He may draw from it divine harmonies' (HF 43). She assures us that a 'praise of glory' – a person whose very life gives glory to God – is 'under the action of the Holy Spirit who effects everything in her' (HF 44). And she also says to her sister, a musician like herself: 'the Holy Spirit will transform you into a mysterious lyre, which, in silence, beneath His divine touch, will produce a magnificent canticle to Love' (L 269).

Elizabeth speaks, too, of receiving the Spirit in terms of water – the living water (cf. John 4.10): 'Oh, how powerful over souls is the apostle who remains always at the Spring of living waters,' she writes to a missionary; 'then he can overflow without his soul ever becoming empty, since he lives in communion with the Infinite!' (L 124). This is a perfect expression of Thérèse's longing for God to fill her emptiness with himself; for her *infinite desires* (LT 107) to be met by the only One who could ever fulfil them perfectly: the Infinite. Elizabeth writes also to a priest: 'that the Spirit of Love . . . may pour Himself out upon you in overflowing measure' (L 193; cf. L 214). It is the teaching of St Paul: 'God's love has been poured into our hearts through the Holy Spirit who has been given to us' (Rom.

5.5). And this love, animating us from within, is there to guide us at every moment of our life.

The Spirit guiding us in our daily life

> When the Spirit of truth comes, he will guide you into all truth; for he will not speak on his own authority, but whatever he hears he will speak, and he will declare to you the things that are to come.
>
> (John 16.13)

Voices of the Spirit

When Teresa took up her pen to speak about prayer, she never failed to commend herself and her writing to the Holy Spirit: 'I really need to entrust myself, as I've already done, to the Holy Spirit and beg Him to speak for me' (IC IV:1:1), she says. With characteristic humility she prays that the Lord 'be pleased that I manage to explain something about these very difficult things [the prayer of union]'; and she adds: 'I know well that this will be impossible if His Majesty and the Holy Spirit do not move my pen' (IC V:4:11). One of the most stunning examples of this took place on the eve of the feast of the Trinity in 1577. Wanting to know how she should go about writing a treatise on prayer, which she had been asked to do, she was suddenly shown by God 'a most beautiful crystal globe, made in the shape of a castle, and containing seven mansions, in the seventh and innermost of which was the King of Glory'.[1] And so she began to write the book that would become *The Interior Castle*.[2]

It was likewise the Spirit at work in Teresa when she said, concerning her autobiography: 'God enlightened my intellect' as he 'wanted to say what I neither was able nor knew how to say' (*Life* 18:8). We cannot help but recall those words of St Paul about the Spirit helping us in our prayer, interceding for us 'when we do not know how to pray as we ought' (Rom. 8.26). Once the Holy Spirit intervenes on our behalf, our prayer and our words take on a singular power and depth. This is a hallmark of the Carmelite saints, for they are people of prayer who open themselves without reserve to the Spirit's transforming action. The saints invite us, by sharing with us their own experience of praying in the Spirit (cf. *Life* 18:8), to explore more deeply the mysteries revealed and concealed in the word of God.

Without the noise of words

We can so easily forget that it is only through the gift of the Spirit that the risen Jesus is present, working silently in our hearts and in the Church. It is no doubt for this reason that the saints do not always feel the need to mention the Spirit *explicitly*. The Holy Spirit teaches noiselessly in a most delicate and subtle way – inspiring, prompting, suggesting, and inviting a free response: 'Where the Spirit of the Lord is, there is freedom' (2 Cor. 3.17).

So gentle, quiet and imperceptible are these inspirations of the Spirit that we may never be fully conscious of them. Teresa herself evokes the Gospel image of the good shepherd to explain the delicacy of God's action through his Spirit, drawing ever more deeply into his mystery those who pray. The Spirit of Jesus, she tells us, acts like 'a good shepherd, with a whistle so gentle that even they themselves almost fail to hear it' (IC IV:3:2).

St Thérèse gives us two remarkable examples of the Spirit working 'without the noise of words', as she expresses it. Here, she speaks explicitly of Jesus – but we can see implicitly that it is the Spirit of Jesus at work in her as she explains:

> I understand and I know from experience that: '*The kingdom of God is within you.*' Jesus has no need of books or teachers to instruct souls; He teaches without the noise of words. Never have I heard Him speak, but I feel that He is within me at each moment; He is guiding and inspiring me with what I must say and do. I find just when I need them certain lights that I had not seen until then, and it isn't most frequently during my hours of prayer that these are most abundant but rather in the midst of my daily occupations. (SS, p. 179; cf. Luke 17.21)

What we refer to as the 'sacrament of the present moment' could be applied perfectly to this passage, and perhaps even more so to the next. In this second well-known passage, Thérèse speaks of the hidden and mysterious action of God that 'nourishes' her with his guidance through the Spirit in the depths of her heart. She writes:

> I have frequently noticed that Jesus doesn't want me to lay up *provisions*; He nourishes me at each moment with a totally new food; I find it within me without my knowing how it is there. I believe it is Jesus Himself hidden in the depths of my poor little heart: He is giving me the grace of acting within me, making me think of all He desires me to do at the present moment. (SS, p. 165)

Enlightened at the proper time

The 'spiritual' sense of Scripture

Our Carmelite saints give us some privileged insights into the action of the Spirit in the light of the Scriptures. One of the most helpful writers in this respect is John of the Cross. He writes of what is known as the 'spiritual' sense of Scripture, or what we might call 'spiritual truths', as in this passage from St Paul who says that the word of God 'is not taught by human wisdom but taught by the Spirit, interpreting spiritual truths to those who possess the Spirit' (1 Cor. 2.13). As John of the Cross shows us, this spiritual sense of Scripture has a solid basis in the promise of the Holy Spirit who will guide the Church 'into all truth' (John 16.13). John writes:

> God usually affirms, teaches, and promises many things, not so there will be an immediate understanding of them, but so that afterward at the proper time, or when the effect is produced, one may receive light about them. (2A 20:3)

The point John is highlighting is that the words of Christ may not at first seem clear to us, just as with the disciples. But 'at the proper time', the Spirit will remind them of what Jesus has said, and they will understand the relevance of those words for their life and mission (cf. John 14.26; 2.22; 12.16).[3] John also goes on to say that when the right time had come for the disciples to preach the message of Christ, 'the Holy Spirit descended on them'. And he continues: 'The Holy Spirit was to explain to them, as Christ affirmed, all that he had taught them during his life' (2A 20:3). What this shows is that God chooses, as and when the time is right, according to his plan, *when* to enlighten us.

In mystery and concealment

The Spirit is associated, however, not just with enlightenment and disclosure, but also with a providential concealment and sense of mystery. Echoing St Paul's words, John of the Cross refers to the 'groanings' of the Spirit, as in this passage:

> It would be foolish to think that expressions of love arising from mystical understanding . . . are fully explainable. The Spirit of the Lord, who abides in us and aids our weakness, as St Paul says, pleads for us with unspeakable groanings in order to manifest what we can

> neither fully understand nor comprehend . . . the Holy Spirit, unable to
> express the fullness of his meaning in ordinary words, utters mysteries
> in strange figures and likenesses. (SC Prol.1; cf. Rom. 8.26)

Here, we gain a sense of something that is meant to elude our understanding, yet in which we can and should trust. This role of the Spirit
– fostering concealment and mystery – has the effect of evoking in
us an ever deeper disposition of faith.

This sense of mystery and concealment, or of revelation that
is only gradual – held back until 'the proper time' – has been
highlighted here, before we move on to the great role of the Spirit
in revealing God to us. For it is important to keep in mind that,
however much we find ourselves enlightened and strengthened,
we are mere human beings, incapable of knowing anything of
God's inner life and action, or of his future plans for us, if he did
not choose to reveal it. The more we receive – were we even to be
shown the highest heavens like St Paul himself (cf. 2 Cor. 12.2) –
the humbler we should feel. As Teresa writes: 'It ordinarily happens
when I receive some favour from the Lord that I am first humbled
within myself so that I might see more clearly how far I am from
deserving favours' (*Life* 38:17).

The Spirit revealing God to us

> [The Spirit] will glorify me, for he will take what is mine and declare it
> to you. All that the Father has is mine; therefore I said that he will take
> what is mine and declare it to you. (John 16.14–15)

'Infinite horizons'

The Spirit 'will take what is mine and declare it to you,' Jesus says
twice to his disciples (John 16.13–14), so emphasizing this important
role of the Spirit. Up until now, we have looked at how the Spirit
enlightens us in our daily lives and also reveals to us 'the things that
are to come' (John 16.13). We are now going to look at how God
reveals *himself* to us – opening up to us, in Jesus, the inner life of the
Blessed Trinity – and, even more than this, how he *shares* this life
with us, drawing us into the whole dynamic movement of the Three
Persons. The Carmelite saints, with their own personal insights, help
us to understand this great mystery and how to enter more deeply
into it.

Thérèse repeats this lesson in her own simple way when, speaking of Scripture, she says: 'a single word uncovers for my soul infinite horizons' (LT 226). She is echoing, with her own original touch, the teaching of St Paul, who himself has been shown the infinite horizons (cf. 2 Cor. 12.2). Paul writes:

> What no eye has seen, nor ear heard, nor has entered into the human heart, what God has prepared for those who love him, God has revealed to us through the Spirit. For the Spirit searches everything, even the depths of God . . . No one comprehends the thoughts of God except the Spirit of God. (1 Cor. 2.9–11; cf. Isa. 64.4)

The 'divine company'

In telling the story of her life, Teresa speaks of a mystical experience in which she 'saw the most sacred humanity' – that is, the humanity of Jesus – and was shown that it 'was taken into the bosom of the Father' (*Life* 38:17). This was a most privileged insight into the communion of the Father and the Son, as revealed in God's word: 'The only Son, who is *in the bosom of the Father*, he has made him known' (John 1.18).

To be *in Jesus*, then, is to be *with him where he is* – in union with his Father – and, at one with Jesus, to be *drawn by the Spirit into the inner life of the Blessed Trinity*. Teresa invites us to enter, with awe, into her experience of God as the Three, and into a sharing in the dialogue and ceaseless exchange of love in the inner life of God. When she speaks of the highest form of prayer, she shares with us one of her most profound mystical experiences – a vision of the three Persons of the Trinity – and their presence within us:

> [In this highest union with God] all three Persons communicate themselves to [the soul], speak to it, and explain those words of the Lord in the Gospel: that He and the Father and the Holy Spirit will come to dwell with the soul that loves Him and keeps His commandments. Oh, God help me! How different is hearing and believing these words from understanding their truth in this way! Each day this soul becomes more amazed, for these Persons never seem to leave it any more, but it clearly beholds, in the way that was mentioned, that they are within it. In the extreme interior, in some place very deep within itself, the nature of which it doesn't know how to explain, because of a lack of learning, it perceives this divine company. (IC VII:1:6–7; cf. Sp Test 13; John 14.23)

Heart to heart

In a quite remarkable parallel, Elizabeth of the Trinity would also receive an intimate manifestation of the Holy Trinity. This experience, occurring just a few months before she died, crowned Elizabeth's life of persevering recollection and ceaseless prayer. One morning, the feast of the Ascension in 1906, she exclaimed to her prioress:

> The good God has granted me such a favour that I have lost all idea of time. Early this morning I heard within the depths of my soul the sentence: 'If anyone loves Me . . . My Father will love him, and We will come to him, and will make Our abode with him', and at the same instant I realized its truth. I could not tell you how the Three Divine Persons revealed Themselves, but I saw Them, holding their counsel of love within me, and I seem to see Them still. Oh! how great God is, and how He loves us![4]

One very interesting aspect of these two mystical experiences is that when God revealed himself in this way, both Teresa and Elizabeth heard, as it were, the very same passage of Scripture (John 14.23) – one in which Jesus tells us that the three Persons of the Trinity dwell within us. As before, when we looked at the way in which the Spirit brings the words of Jesus back to the memory of the disciples, when they are ready to understand the full import of the words, here we see that Jesus' message about the divine indwelling is brought back to the memory of Teresa and Elizabeth as they contemplate, through their vision, the very real way in which the Trinity dwells within the soul. In each case, it is the culmination of a lifetime adoring the presence of the Trinity in the darkness of faith – it is, for them, the right time: when they have become ready to receive this message in such a direct way.

These experiences bring home to us, as mentioned earlier, that God does not just give us guidance – as if he were purely a heavenly spiritual director – but most of all wishes to reveal God to us, and share with us the divine life.

Desire for God

Longings too deep for words

We cannot long for what we do not know. So every time we feel a desire for God, he has already been made known to us, even if we are not conscious of how he was revealed to us. In fact, it is through the action of the Holy Spirit, for one of the roles of the Spirit is to *increase our desire for God.*

It does not matter that we are weak, inadequate, fragile. Despite all this, Teresa insists on the importance of having great desires for God. They are inseparably linked with her emphasis on determination and a wholehearted commitment to prayer. For her, there are wonders hidden in the human heart: powerful longings too deep for words. Or, to recall a famous passage from St Paul: 'The Spirit himself intercedes for us with sighs too deep for words' (Rom. 8.26). These 'sighs', these 'longings', represent our most profound desires and need to be seen in this light. Only the Spirit, then, can give expression to our deepest desires for God – so profound that we may not even be fully aware of them.

Teresa has rightly been hailed by the poet Richard Crashaw as an 'undaunted daughter of desires'.[5] She was astonished at just how much can be done if only we have the courage to attempt great things for God. An insatiable longing for God had been her desire from childhood when she set off with her brother Rodrigo, in the hope of being martyred by the Moors. Her parents were distraught with fear. But when she was eventually found, she simply explained to them: 'I went because I want to see God, and to see Him we must die.'[6]

In this way, Teresa was already echoing, unwittingly, the deepest aspirations of every human heart, fragile, restless and vulnerable. There is pain beyond all telling, hidden in the heart of love. It is there, too, in the heart of prayer – a thirst, and a longing unsatisfied, a reaching out in love of a heart that is always restless until it rests in God, to use a well-known phrase from St Augustine. The Psalmist captures this longing beautifully:

> . . . my soul is yearning
> for you, my God.
> My soul is thirsting for God . . .
>
> O God, you are my God, for you I long;
> for you my soul is thirsting.
> My body pines for you
> like a dry, weary land without water.
>
> (Ps. 41.2–3; 62.2)

A fling of the heart

Thérèse's teaching on prayer is also inseparably linked with these great desires inspired by the Spirit. As we have already seen, she gives us a brief, but striking, description of prayer as 'an aspiration of the heart' (SS, p. 242).[7] 'To aspire' means, literally, 'to breathe towards' (from *spirare* and *ad*) – to long, or to sigh, or to yearn for *something* or *someone*. In a word, it is *to desire*. When the object is God, it is the ultimate outburst of love – a fling of the heart to the heart of God. But here, we begin to see the originality and depth of Thérèse's understanding of these deep longings for God. For her, as we shall now see, they are inseparably linked with weakness.

Thérèse shows us that doing great things for God, and wanting to do great things for God, actually comes from acknowledging and accepting our littleness and weakness. This, she confesses repeatedly, is essential for all who wish to follow her path of spiritual childhood, or 'Little Way' as she called it: 'Is there a soul more *little*, more powerless than mine?' (SS, p. 193), she asks; 'I am the smallest of creatures; I know my misery and my feebleness' (SS, p. 195). All these facets of Thérèse's teaching are summed up in one important sentence:

> I feel that if You found a soul weaker and littler than mine . . . You would be pleased to grant it still greater favours, provided it abandoned itself with total confidence to Your Infinite Mercy.   (SS, p. 200)

The significance of these words is the relationship of cause and effect: the littler the soul, the greater the divine favours. And Thérèse will go even further, seeing herself as 'nothingness' – which, she sees, will draw down the Spirit of God so as to 'transform this nothingness into *fire*' (SS, p. 195).

Yes, in her 'extreme littleness' (SS, p. 198), Thérèse experiences 'great aspirations' (SS, p. 197), 'measureless desires' (SS, p. 197), '*infinite desires*' (LT 107), 'desires and longings which reach even unto infinity' (SS, p. 192). She was confused by this and asked the question: 'O Jesus, my Love, my Life, how can I combine these contrasts?' (SS, p. 192). It is a question that we, too, can explore with great profit, as we look now to the meaning of her 'Little Way'.

Capacity for the Infinite

The remarkable thing about the 'Little Way' – and this cannot be overemphasized – is what we might term a 'holy paradox'. The vast desires of Thérèse sprang from the experience of her own power-lessness and weakness. In fact, the deeper she plunged into the abyss of her own littleness, the greater and more intense her desires became, and the more confusing: after all, how can someone who feels so little and so powerless aspire to be a great saint for God? This was the crux – and the pain – of her longing. But then the Spirit enlightened her: just as a child at the foot of the stairs, too small to climb them by herself, is carried by her mother or father, Thérèse realized that her littleness gave her all the greater claim on God's mercy. The staircase became a lift! Desires that seemed impossible became – through God's carrying her – completely realizable.

John of the Cross sheds further light on what is happening in this paradox of desire. Speaking of the 'deep caverns' of the human spirit – its faculties of memory, intellect and will – he writes that 'anything less than the infinite fails to fill them' (LF 3:18). And he further observes: 'capable of infinite goods . . . they cannot receive these infinite goods until they are completely empty' (LF 3:18). St Augustine repeats the same lesson: 'This is our life, to be exercised by desire. But we are exercised by holy desire only in so far as we have cut off our longings from the love of the world . . . empty that which is to be filled.'[8] It was precisely this emptying out of herself, this entering into the profound depths of her own weakness, neediness and nothingness, that put Thérèse in touch with her vast desires, her sheer emptiness and capacity for God, for the infinite.

For Thérèse, to be in touch with her humanity – her weakness, her total dependence on God – was to know herself as needy. And as she entered the depths of her own littleness and powerlessness, so Thérèse experienced her *total capacity for God*, released in the vast hunger and yearning of her painful desires, which only an infinite God of love could activate and fully satisfy. Thérèse saw herself as an immense and limitless capacity for God, and it was precisely her unsatisfied desires that impelled her forward in absolute confidence and trust towards the promised gift of God himself.

At first, Thérèse seemed troubled by her vast desires. But all that changed as they gave meaning to her experience of endless need: for they revealed to her the transcendent aspect of what it means to be made for God: fully human in her endless desire and in her openness to be filled with God's love. For to know our neediness – something that mostly we prefer not to embrace – is in fact to rely, like Thérèse, unreservedly on God's merciful love. It is to believe that, with God, all things are possible (cf. Luke 1.37) – even in our own lives.

It is not, however, will power but faith, impelled by the Spirit, that gives us the belief to know, as Thérèse did, that her own 'nothingness' could be transformed into *'fire'* (SS, p. 195). No image can convey more strikingly the powerful flame of the Spirit. The more he inflames us, the more we long to be united with God, so desire for God is very much a fruit of the work of the Spirit within us. It is no coincidence, then, that desire is often expressed – as it was by Thérèse – as 'aspiration'. It is a breathing towards God with the breath of the Spirit.

The work of transformation

'Come upon me'

We come now to what we might call the crux of the work of the Spirit in us: his action within us to transform us into the likeness of Christ. This is expressed perfectly by Elizabeth of the Trinity as the Spirit's 'creative Action' – and at its heart, this is the work of the entire Trinity within us.

As Elizabeth saw so well and expressed in her *Prayer to the Trinity*, the annunciation to the Virgin Mary is the perfect example and the summit of this action: the Father sending the Spirit, so that Christ would be born in her. This, in fact, reflects what happens in *us* when we are open to the action of the Spirit: he is sent into us by the Father, so that Christ may be born in us. 'It is Christ that lives in me' (Gal. 2.20), writes St Paul. And for Carmelites – whose prayer, we have seen, is rooted in relationship – this Trinitarian action is a stimulus to prayer: Elizabeth relates to *the Father bending over her, the Spirit coming upon her, and Christ dwelling within her*. This awareness needs to accompany our own prayer, too, when we open ourselves to the Spirit's action and pray, like Elizabeth: 'O consuming Fire, Spirit of Love, "come upon me" . . .' (PT; cf. Luke 1.35). These words are themselves an invitation to us to surrender, as Mary did, to the action of the Holy Spirit, so that Christ's life may grow in us. It is to ask to be transformed into the likeness of Christ, whereby we become 'another humanity' for him, as Elizabeth expresses it, in which his whole life may be lived out in us, too.

The incarnation of Christ at the annunciation – the action of the Spirit, the gift of the Son by his Father – is, then, an experience of the Trinity. So Elizabeth's prayer opens up the inner life of the Three, in which we are all invited to share. The three heavenly Guests within our soul are always sharing and communing with each other in the depths of our heart, and this exchange of love is an unceasing dialogue. It is an active presence, creative, always reaching out to give, to communicate itself – and it is happening at every moment!

Sharing the life of the Three

To perceive, through faith, this amazing truth – that the Trinity dwells within us – will inevitably make us want to respond. This is already a sign that our hearts are under the action of the Holy Spirit. And as we are led to respond, in a dialogue of prayer, it happens – even without our being aware of it – that we are becoming ever more open to transformation. It happens, quite simply, because the channels of communication have been opened up. Elizabeth writes:

> may the Holy Spirit, who is Love, make your heart a little hearth that rejoices the Three Divine Persons through the ardour of its flames . . . Oh! how our soul needs to draw strength in prayer, doesn't it, especially in that intimate heart-to-heart in which the soul flows into God and God flows into it to transform it into Himself.   (L 278)

John of the Cross, in what is now a classic description of trans-formative prayer, enters yet further into the mystery of the divine life. He highlights the role of the Holy Spirit as *the means of communication* both between God and the soul, and within the inner life of the Trinity. He refers to the Spirit, appropriately, in terms of breath or 'spiration':

> By his divine breath-like spiration, the Holy Spirit elevates the soul sublimely and informs her and makes her capable of breathing in God the same spiration of love that the Father breathes in the Son and the Son in the Father. This spiration of love is the Holy Spirit himself, who in the Father and the Son breathes out to her in this transformation in order to unite her to himself . . . In the transformation that the soul possesses in this life, the same spiration passes from God to the soul and from the soul to God with notable frequency and blissful love, although not in the open and manifest degree proper to the next life.
> (SC 39:3–4; cf. L 185)

This passage by John of the Cross brings to mind the well-known icon of the Trinity by Rublëv. The Three Persons are seated around a table, in perfect, indissoluble union with each other. But do we not perceive a spare place at the table in the foreground? This is where each individual believer may take his or her place, communing with the Father, Son and Holy Spirit through the very breath of the Spirit. 'The flame of divine life *touches* the soul,' writes Edith Stein, who describes the fruit of this divine touch: '[the soul] dissolves wholly in love' (Sci Cr, p. 188; cf. LF 1:8).

How could anyone *not* be changed, when in direct contact with God himself? Yes, prayer is the key, for it is the activity of communing with him. And love is the fruit. Elizabeth of the Trinity, who found John's teaching on spiritual transformation nothing less than life-changing, explains perfectly what it means to be transformed in love: it is, she would say, recalling the words of St Paul, to be 'conformed to the image of [the] Son' (Rom. 8.29; cf. L 304). For this reason, one of the main fruits of transformation in prayer is strength in illness and in other trials – in the image of *Jesus as he lived his passion*. For Elizabeth, in the last year of her life, this was her programme for Lent.

Strengthened to bear witness

'So much strength in suffering'

'Before I die, I dream of being transformed into Jesus Crucified, and that gives me so much strength in suffering' (L 324). Elizabeth wrote these words while in the throes of the then incurable Addison's disease, which for the last few months of her life caused her the most enormous suffering: severe headaches and nausea, the inability to eat, an almost total insomnia, excruciating inflammation throughout her entire body. So dreadful were her sufferings that, even though she longed to be associated in Christ's work of redemption, at times she knew what it was to feel suicidal (cf. L 329, n. 2). But faced with all this, she allowed love to transform her suffering, which in turn transformed Elizabeth herself.

Elizabeth had the desire to love Christ 'even unto death' (PT), and her love embraced the whole Body of Christ spread out in the world. At the height of her agony, she was able to pray: 'Spend all my substance for Your glory, let it distil drop by drop for Your Church.'[9]

This was Elizabeth's way of identifying totally with these words of St Paul she so loved: 'Now I rejoice in my sufferings for your sake, and in my flesh I complete what is lacking in Christ's afflictions for the sake of his body, that is, the church' (Col. 1.24; cf. L 309; GV 7).

With Christ on the cross

Thérèse, too, at times felt tempted to suicide, due to her overwhelming sufferings; but like Elizabeth, she was strengthened by the Spirit, and overcame this temptation with her love of God and her desire to help the world through her suffering. After a protracted illness, tuberculosis, when Thérèse felt she could take no more, she said to the prioress who was at her bedside, 'I assure you, the chalice is filled to the brim! . . . But God is not going to abandon me, I'm sure . . . He has never abandoned me' (LC, p. 205; r.e.). These words were uttered on the day of her death – the ultimate trust. One eyewitness would write of those final moments:

> For more than two hours, a terrible rattle tore her chest. Her face was blue, her hands purplish, her feet were cold, and she shook in all her members. Perspiration stood out in enormous drops on her forehead and rolled down her cheeks. Her difficulties in breathing were always increasing . . .   (LC, p. 206)

This reads like a description of the crucifixion itself. Her death was like that of Jesus on the cross, in abandonment and total surrender to love – a stark reminder of the hidden workings of the Spirit, bearing witness to Jesus living in Thérèse.

Strength in persecution

One great Carmelite who bore witness to Jesus in a time of persecution was Edith Stein. A Jewish woman in Germany, soon after the Nazis took power she offered herself to Jesus to help carry his cross, in whatever way he chose (cf. SEL, p. 17). Nine years later, by then a Carmelite nun, she would die in Auschwitz. We are privileged to have some eyewitness accounts of her final days at Westerbork transit camp, and they show her to be a shining witness to the power of the Spirit bearing witness in her to Christ; 'the Spirit of truth', Jesus had said, '. . . will bear witness to me' (John 15.26) – and, in the example of Edith Stein, we see how the strength of the Spirit bears witness to Christ in those who are persecuted for his sake.

These are the days which Edith spent among her own anguished people in the squalid transit camp. There, she comforted the children and combed their hair; she was calm, prayed continually and consoled others in their distress. One eyewitness, a woman who was later released, described Edith praying in the camp as 'a Pietà without the Christ'[10] – a heartfelt but paradoxical statement, for Christ was indeed there with Edith, living his passion at one with her and deep within her, though invisible to the naked eye. In fact, not quite invisible. Others have testified to the radiant presence all around Edith. One man, working as an official in the camp, described her with these remarkable words:

> one sister . . . impressed me immediately, whose warm, glowing smile has never been erased from my memory . . . From the moment I met her in the camp at Westerbork . . . I knew: here is someone truly great. For a couple of days she lived in that hellhole, walking, talking, and praying . . . like a saint. And she really was one . . . When she spoke, it was impossible not to be moved by her humility and conviction. Talking with her was like . . . journeying into another world, where for the moment, Westerbork ceased to exist.[11]

The strength shown by Elizabeth, Thérèse and Edith, whether in illness or in persecution, bears witness to the power of love, and to the power of God to sustain us in situations which, humanly speaking, are impossible. But there is, of course, an explicit form of witnessing to Christ, and here we have the words of Jesus to remind us of the trials that accompany bearing witness in the work of the Holy Spirit: 'You will be dragged before governors and kings for my sake,' Jesus says to his disciples, 'to bear testimony before them . . . Do not be anxious how you are to speak or what you are to say; for what you are to say will be given to you in that hour; for it is not you who speak, but the Spirit of your Father speaking through you' (Matt. 10.18–20).

The seclusion of the cloister is no guarantee of exemption from persecution, as the example of Edith makes clear. She lived up to the challenge to follow Jesus on the way of his passion and death, but not through her own strength. For Edith, like the followers of Jesus in the Gospels, bore witness explicitly to her belonging to Christ. Edith well knew that Jesus had foretold the persecution of his followers. Questioned by an SS officer in the camp as to her identity, she spontaneously replied: 'I am Catholic' – thus bearing witness to Christ in a profession of faith.[12] It should be noted, here, that the Nazis hated the Catholic Church, and that Edith had been arrested along with the *Catholic* Jews in the Netherlands, in response to the protest of their Archbishop against the Nazis' persecution of Jewish people.

'If the world hates you,' Jesus had warned, 'know that it has hated me before it hated you . . . A servant is not greater than his master. If they persecuted me, they will persecute you . . . They hated me without cause' (John 15.18, 20, 25). In her last days, before her death on 9 August 1942 in the gas chambers of Auschwitz, Edith was at one, in mind and heart, with her suffering Messiah as he lived again in her the conflict between good and evil, truth and error, light and darkness. The light of the Spirit – this mysterious yet intimate Companion – dispels all darkness.

Eternal Love!

No wonder Edith could write this magnificent prayer to the Holy Spirit – a résumé of the life of every Christian led by the gentle yet powerful hand of the Spirit, as we journey through our own Calvary in the dark valley of our exile, towards the glory of the resurrection and the embrace of Eternal Love:

> Who are You, Kindly Light, who fill me now,
> And brighten all the darkness of my heart?
> You guide me forward, like a mother's hand;
> And if You let me go, I could not take a single step alone.
> You are the space embracing all my being, hidden in You.
> Loosened from You, I would fall into the abyss of nothingness
> from which You raised me to the Light.
> Nearer to me than I myself am,
> And more within me than my inmost self,
> You are outside my grasp, beyond my reach.
>   And no name can contain You:
>   You, Holy Spirit,
> You, Eternal Love![13]

Questions for reflection or discussion

1 In what almost imperceptible ways do you find the Holy Spirit guiding you in your daily life?

2 When you are at prayer, what dispositions can you take on, to be totally open to the creative action of the Holy Spirit?

3 What great longings for God, and for the service of God, do you aspire to? Do you really believe that 'nothing is impossible to God' – even in your own life?

Notes

Prologue

1 In like manner, references in this book to 'Carmelites' (apart from historical instances) are to all readers who wish to enrich their spirituality with the Carmelite charism. For further details of the origins of the Carmelite order, see Chapter 1, the section 'The birthplace of Carmel'.

2 A refrain which runs all through a beautiful poem of John of the Cross (P 7), known as 'El Pastorcico' ('The Little Shepherd Boy').

1 The Carmelite *Rule*

1 See this most relevant passage from a recent Church document: 'Following Christ, as proposed in the Gospel, is . . . the "supreme rule" of all the institutes. One of the earliest names for monastic life is "evangelical life" . . . In the rule of the Carmelites, the fundamental precept is that of "meditating on the Law of the Lord day and night", in order to translate it into concrete action: "all that you must do, do it in the word of the Lord"', in Congregation for Institutes of Consecrated Life and Societies of Apostolic Life, *Keep Watch! – Year of Consecrated Life: A Letter to Consecrated Men and Women Journeying in the Footsteps of God*. Catholic Truth Society, London, 2014, § 8, pp. 38 and 40.

2 Cf. DO, vol. I, pp. [30–1] (*sic*).

3 The following of Christ is the 'fundamental norm' and 'supreme law' of the consecrated life, in that it is the essence of the whole Christian life: see Vatican II, *Perfectae Caritatis* (*Decree on the Appropriate Renewal of the Religious Life*), § 2.

4 Edith Stein, a Carmelite saint of Jewish origin attuned to the Hebrew Scriptures, considers this phrase in the *Rule* and asks the question: 'What is meant by "the Law of the Lord"?' She refers to Psalm 118 as being 'entirely filled with the command to know the Law and to be led by it through life' and explains: 'The Psalmist was certainly thinking of the Law of the Old Covenant . . . But the Lord has freed us from the yoke of this Law. We can consider the Saviour's great commandment of love, which he says includes the whole Law and the Prophets, as the Law of the New Covenant . . . But we understand the Law of the New Covenant, even better, to be the Lord himself' (HL, p. 4).

5 This point is well made by Dom O. Rousseau's article 'The Call to Perfection in Patristic Tradition', *Vocation* (*Religious Life*, II). Blackfriars, London, 1952, pp. 8–9.

6 See my article, 'The Temptations of Jesus: An Exodus Experience', *Mount Carmel*, vol. 61, no. 1, 2013, pp. 18–26.

7 See *Rule*, § 18–19. For Paul's metaphor for *putting on* Christ and being transformed in him through baptism, see Gal. 3.27; Rom. 13.14; Col. 3.10; Eph. 4.24.

8 In the eleventh century, Western Europe experienced a renewal of eremitical life and an extensive religious movement with the aim of following Christ in his poverty. Its adherents called themselves 'The Poor of Christ'. People resolutely renounced the world in order to dedicate themselves totally to God in a life of penitence. Pilgrimages to the Holy Land were regarded as the high point of the penitential life, and the hermits of Mount Carmel were part of this movement. See K. Waaijman O Carm, *The Mystical Space of Carmel: A Commentary on the Carmelite Rule*. Peeters (The Fiery Arrow Collection), Leuven, 1999, pp. 2 and 7.

9 The *Catechism of the Catholic Church* (§ 2563) explains well the biblical meaning of 'heart'. See also Thomas Merton's *Contemplative Prayer*. Darton, Longman & Todd, London, 1968, pp. 22, 34 and 38.

10 Women first joined Carmel as oblates; an example is known of this in 1283. The first cloisters of Carmelite nuns, however, date from the fifteenth century, founded under the reform of the order by Blessed John Soreth: see J. Smet O Carm, *Cloistered Carmel: A Brief History of the Carmelite Nuns*. Institutum Carmelitanum, Rome, 1986, pp. 11 and 25.

2 The heritage of Elijah

1 That is, reformers of the Order of Carmel, even though they are also founders of the 'Teresian' or 'Discalced' Carmel. See, for example, this explanation by Edith Stein: 'Our Holy Mother strenuously denied that she was founding a new Order. She wanted nothing except to reawaken the original spirit of the old Rule [of St Albert]' (HL, p. 1). See also M. Blake OCD, 'Teresa of Avila: Her Vocation as Foundress', *Mount Carmel*, vol. 63, no. 4, 2015, pp. 18–23.

2 The inspiration of Elijah for the Order of Carmel was first stated in its Constitutions of 1281: in the opening lines, now known as the *Rubrica Prima*. This was the Carmelites' first recorded attempt at defining their identity, and their conviction appeared in the opening paragraphs of constitution after constitution for hundreds of years; see J. Ackerman, *Elijah: Prophet of Carmel*. ICS Publications, Washington, DC, 2003, pp. 122–3. For a helpful discussion of the Carmelite Order's search for identity, see W. McGreal O Carm, *At the Fountain of Elijah: The Carmelite Tradition*. Darton, Longman & Todd, London, 1999, pp. 37–48.

3 See also Chapter 4, the section 'An inflow of God'.

4 Ackerman treats well the relevance, the difficulties and the challenge of the ancient prophet Elijah for present-day readers of his story: see her *Elijah*, pp. 1–31. See also K. Healy O Carm, *Prophet of Fire*. Institutum Carmelitanum, Rome, 1990. Note also two issues of *Mount Carmel*, devoted either fully or in part to the many and various aspects of Elijah's story and their relation to the Carmelite charism: see *Mount Carmel*, vol. 51, no. 3, 2003, and vol. 56, no. 2, 2008.

5 Note that Teresa of Avila uses an almost identical expression in *The Interior Castle*, her work on the dwelling places of the soul; the venomous creatures she mentions are, of course, the obstacles in the *outer* dwelling places of the castle (cf. IC I:2:14).

6 From her 'Bookmark' prayer (poem 9 in volume 3 of her *Collected Works*).

7 This is to pray like Jesus, who 'stands, always and everywhere, before the face of God' (HL, p. 12). Two other quotations from Edith Stein show that she describes the Carmelite vocation, based on the prayer of Elijah, in very similar and profoundly contemplative terms: 'To stand before the face of the living God – that is our vocation' (HL, p. 1); 'Prayer is looking up into the face of the Eternal' (HL, p. 3).

8 In an early Carmelite document, known sometimes as the *Institution of the First Monks*, this experience at Cherith is used to present Elijah as an exemplar of the monastic and eremitical life: see Book 1, in the foundational work by Felip Ribot O Carm, *The Ten Books on the Way of Life and Great Deeds of the Carmelites*, ed. and tr. R. Copsey O Carm. Saint Albert's Press, Faversham, and Edizioni Carmelitane, Rome, 2005.

9 See William Nicholson's *Shadowlands: A Play*. Samuel French, London, 1990, Act II, p. 41.

10 See Dietrich Bonhoeffer's *Christology*. Collins, London, and Harper & Row, New York, 1966, p. 27.

11 From 'A Letter to John Dryden', in James McAuley's *Collected Poems 1936–1970*. Angus & Robertson, Sydney, 1971, p. 94. For the copyright acknowledgement, see p. 87.

12 See Patrick Kavanagh's poem 'From Failure Up', which admirably conveys the sense of seeing the whole of one's life's achievements as nothing but 'rubble': in *Patrick Kavanagh: The Complete Poems*. The Peter Kavanagh Hand Press, New York, and The Goldsmith Press, Newbridge, 1972, p. 161.

13 Horeb is referred to as 'the mountain of God' (cf. Exod. 3.1); it is another name for Mount Sinai on which the Lord gave the Ten Commandments to Moses.

14 This is, literally, 'a sound of thin silence', one of the various suggested translations of this rich phrase: see C. E. Morrison O Carm, 'Handing on the Mantle: The Transmission of the Elijah Cycle in the Biblical Versions', in K. J. Egan T O Carm and C. E. Morrison O Carm (eds), *Master of the*

Sacred Page: Essays and Articles in Honor of Roland E. Murphy, O.Carm., on the Occasion of his Eightieth Birthday. The Carmelite Institute, Washington, DC, 1997, pp. 109–29 (especially pp. 112–18).

15 For an excellent treatment of prayer, and particularly the prayer of silence, see M. McCormack OCD, *Upon This Mountain: Prayer in the Carmelite Tradition.* Teresian Press, Oxford, 2009, pp. 42–50.

16 See also the prophecy about Elijah's return, in Malachi 4.5–6 (RSV)/3.23–24 (Jerusalem Bible).

17 Compare with the translation in the Jerusalem Bible: 'you scourge of Israel'. For a discussion of the *Rule* and spiritual combat, see Chapter 1, the section 'The strength of a fragile Church'.

18 The main purpose of Elijah in this episode was not to shed the blood of these false prophets – a gesture comprehensible only within the religious framework of his time – but to obtain the conversion of the people. This incident must never be used to justify slaughter or even intolerance, directed in the name of religion against people at variance with one's beliefs and convictions. Ackerman comments: 'For centuries readers have remembered and retold the most dramatic parts of [Elijah's] old story, such as the holocaust on [Mount] Carmel or Elijah's ascension into heaven. However, in his oldest tale found in 1–2 Kings, what matters most about Elijah are the results of such powerful experiences, not the spectacular events themselves. These and everything else in that story knit his people to God.' See Ackerman, *Elijah*, p. 31.

3 Reading the Scriptures with Mary

1 From his lecture 'In the Spirit and Strength of Elias', given at the Catholic University in Washington, summer 1935: see Titus Brandsma, *The Beauty of Carmel.* Clonmore & Reynolds, Dublin, and Burns, Oates & Washbourne, London, 1955, p. 32.

2 These stages are: *reading, meditating* (or pondering), *praying* and *contemplating*; a fifth stage, *action*, which follows on from these four traditional stages, can also be added, as it is here. For an excellent treatment of *lectio divina*, see M. Magrassi OSB, *Praying the Bible: An Introduction to Lectio Divina.* The Liturgical Press, Collegeville, Minn., 1998.

3 See the excellent chapter 'Into Stillness' in M. McCormack OCD, *Upon This Mountain: Prayer in the Carmelite Tradition.* Teresian Press, Oxford, 2009, pp. 42–50.

4 From the Latin words *ob* and *audire*.

4 Teresian spirituality

1 'Mental prayer', as the term suggests, involves engaging the mind through awareness. The opposite would be reciting prayers in a mindless way (which Teresa would say is not real prayer, anyway).

2 See B. F. Westcott, *The Gospel According to St. John*. James Clarke & Co.,
London, 1958, p. 15.

3 Westcott, *The Gospel According to St. John*, p. 15. John also describes
Jesus as being 'towards' (*pros*) the Father in John 1.1, 2.

4 See W. Harrington OP, *Mark*. Veritas (New Testament Message, vol. 4),
Dublin, 1979, p. 15.

5 The faculties are known traditionally as the intellect, memory and will.
On the prayer of recollection, see E. McCaffrey OCD, 'Praying with St
Teresa – 3: The Prayer of Companionship', *Mount Carmel*, vol. 46, no.
4, 1999, pp. 9–14. See also two recent articles by Julienne McLean on
Francisco de Osuna, who was an important influence on Teresa in the
area of the prayer of recollection: *Mount Carmel*, vol. 62, no. 4, 2014, pp.
60–6, and vol. 63, no. 1, 2015, pp. 46–53.

6 See Thomas Aquinas' *Summa Theologica* IIa-IIae, q. 180 art. 1 and 7. See
also the explanation by John of the Cross, discussed in Chapter 2 (the
section 'Man of prayer, man of action'), of contemplation as receiving
God's gift of himself.

5 His heart an open wound

1 [Posselt], Sister Teresia de Spiritu Sancto OCD, *Edith Stein*. Sheed &
Ward, London and New York, 1952, p. 64.

2 [Posselt], *Edith Stein*, p. 59.

3 For an excellent discussion of Thérèse's experience of suffering in her
life, and the inspiration she took from Isaiah's portrayal of the Suffering
Servant, see V. O'Hara OCD, '"His face was as though hidden": St
Thérèse's Understanding of Suffering', *Mount Carmel*, vol. 48, no. 4, 2001,
pp. 25–33.

4 In the poem 'From Failure Up' in *Patrick Kavanagh: The Complete
Poems*. The Peter Kavanagh Hand Press, New York, and The Goldsmith
Press, Newbridge, 1972, p. 161. For the copyright acknowledgement, see
p. 87.

5 Curia Generalis OCD (Secretarius pro Monialibus), *To Be a Carmelite
with the Blessed Elizabeth of the Trinity* (Chapter 18 of the series
Guidelines for Study Following the Order Contained in the Declarations).
Discalced Carmelite Order, Rome, n.d., pp. 37–9.

6 A confidence made to Sr Teresa of St Augustine: quoted in PN, p. 184; r.e.

6 Into all truth

1 As told by Fray Diego de Yepes, a priest to whom she recounted this: in
Allison E. Peers (ed. and tr.), *The Complete Works of Saint Teresa of Jesus*,
vol. 2. Sheed & Ward, London, 1946, p. 188.

2 In this work, Teresa expounds the spiritual life in terms of a journey
through seven sets of 'mansions' in the 'interior castle' that is the soul,

at the centre of which God dwells. For an excellent introduction to this work, see E. McCaffrey OCD, *Journey of Love: Teresa of Avila's Interior Castle – A Reader's Guide*. Teresian Press, Oxford, 2015. On the 'prayer of union', see *Journey of Love*, pp. 43ff.

3 For a masterly treatment of these Johannine texts on the action of the Spirit, see I. de La Potterie SJ and S. Lyonnet SJ, *The Christian Lives by the Spirit*. Alba House, New York, 1971, ch. 3, 'The Paraclete', pp. 57–77.

4 *The Praise of Glory: Reminiscences of Sister Elizabeth of the Trinity, A Carmelite Nun of Dijon, 1901–1906*. R & T Washbourne, London, and Benziger Brothers, New York, 1914, pp. 182–3.

5 See Cathleen Medwick, *Teresa of Avila: The Progress of a Soul*. Duckworth, London, 2000, p. 254; the appendix (pp. 251–4) contains the third poem of Crashaw's Teresa cycle.

6 This is not unlike the finding in the Temple of the twelve-year-old Jesus, explaining to an anxious Mary and Joseph that he was called to be 'in [his] Father's house' (Luke 2.49).

7 This description, as seen, has been included in the *Catechism of the Catholic Church* in its opening definition of prayer (cf. § 2558).

8 From the treatise of St Augustine on the First Letter of St John, in DO, vol. I, p. 538. See also, on desire as exercised in prayer, his letter to Proba, in DO, vol. III, pp. 661–2.

9 Office for the Promotion of Causes (ed.), *Elizabeth Still Speaks . . .: In the Processes of Beatification and Canonization*. Carmel of Maria Regina, Eugene, Oreg., 1982, p. 39, § 161.

10 In E. Prégardier and A. Mohr, *Passion im August (2.-9. August 1942): Edith Stein und Gefährtinnen – Weg in Tod und Auferstehung*. Plöger, Annweiler, 1995, p. 52.

11 Account from the Dutch official, Wielek, quoted in W. Herbstrith OCD, *Edith Stein: A Biography*. Ignatius Press, San Francisco, 1992, p. 186. For two other eyewitness accounts, those of P. O. van Kempen and Pierre Cuypers who visited Edith in the camp, see 'Edith Stein and Christian-Jewish Dialogue' in W. Herbstrith OCD (ed.), *Carmelite Studies*, vol. 7 (*Never Forget: Christian and Jewish Perspectives on Edith Stein*). ICS Publications, Washington, DC, 1998, pp. 272–8.

12 See A. Eszer OP, 'Edith Stein, Jewish Catholic Martyr' in J. Sullivan OCD (ed.), *Carmelite Studies*, vol. 4 (*Edith Stein Symposium/Teresian Culture*). ICS Publications, Washington, DC, 1987, p. 317.

13 From Edith's poem 'Seven Rays from a Pentecost Novena'; my translation. See, too, the translation by Waltraut Stein, Edith's great-niece (in HL, p. 141) and also that of Susanne M. Batzdorff, Edith's niece (in SEL, p. 93). Both these versions are accompanied by Edith's German original.

Copyright acknowledgements